KILLING
tea party
PROPAGANDA

KILLING
tea party
PROPAGANDA

STEPHEN BEHRNDT

KILLING TEA PARTY PROPAGANDA

iUniverse books may be ordered through booksellers or by contacting:

iUniverse
1663 Liberty Drive
Bloomington, IN 47403
www.iuniverse.com
1-800-Authors (1-800-288-4677)

ISBN: 978-1-4917-9645-0 (sc)
ISBN: 978-1-4917-9646-7 (e)

Print information available on the last page.

iUniverse rev. date: 06/07/2016

CONTENTS

REACHING THE AGE OF REASON

This book certainly is not a biography but it is a living history of the politics and economic changes of the past 100 years in the USA. If it were a biography I would expect the reader to put it down out of boredom! But, since I have lived through more than 80% of these 100 years on a firsthand up close basis, I can't stop myself from reviewing the events of those years. Before I begin, however, I have to give you an insight into my early years, hopefully to set the foundation of how my outlook and opinions were formed and changed over time. Hopefully the book will deal with aspects of politics, economics, gridlock, the rich & the poor and the hypocrisy of the world we live in today!

I was born in 1934 in Eau Claire, Wisconsin. It was at the height of the Great Depression. Eau Claire had a population of about 48000 people in the late 40's. I was in grade school during the war and entered High school in the late 40's. Eau Claire had a "Teachers College" as we called it, which over the years became a full-fledged branch of the University in Madison. Eau Claire also had a U. S. Rubber Company plant that manufactured auto and truck tires and employed 5000++ workers as I recall. To say the least, to employ over 5000 workers in a town of 48000 people had a great effect on the economy of Eau Claire and the region around it. The birth of a strong middle class was in it's infancy!

The USA had been in the Great Depression since 1929 until WW2 started for the USA when the Japanese bombed Pearl Harbor on December 7th, 1941. Actually WW2 started in September of 1939 when Germany invaded Poland so the war had been going on in Europe for about 27 months before the USA entered the conflict.

During WW2, millions of men went to war, 100's of 1000's of women went to work, many of them in jobs in factories who had not employed female workers "on–the-line" like U. S. Rubber, GM or Ford. Detroit made tanks and jeeps rather than cars. My Dad, who depended on a car for his employment, could not buy a car from 1942 to 1946. Sugar and gasoline were rationed. People were living Spartan lives! It is virtually impossible for me to paint a picture of those times to my Grandchildren! As they stare at their iphones, ipads and send 222 text messages to various friends each day they almost cannot conceive of a world when no one had a TV and people hunched around a radio each night if they could not amuse themselves with reading or talking to each other. More difficult to comprehend was that we had an ICEBOX. Yes, a man would come to our house every few days and put a block of ice into the icebox and that would cool the milk, eggs, butter etc…by convection and conduction. And we were lucky to be able to GET and AFFORD the milk and butter. But my family was not poor! In fact, we lived in a very nice house that my Dad had built for less than $7000.00 in the middle 30's. Please note that I am not complaining. For me, life was great! Like many young people of any generation, I thought this was exactly the way the world went around. Everyone lived this way. On top of that, we were at war!

Then, in the Spring of 1945, the Germans surrendered. We called it Victory in Europe (VE day) followed by Victory in Japan(VJ day) a few months later after we had bombed

Hiroshima and Nagasaki with the first and only atomic weapons ever used in warfare.

Things were going to evolve in Eau Claire and the nation as a whole as WW2 ended. Starting in late 1945, thru the 40's, 50's, 60's and into the 70's America was going to become *thee* world power. Japan, China, Russia, most all of Europe, especially Germany and Italy and many other parts of the world had been devastated. We had lost over a million fighting men in the war and we will never forget them! We had been attacked and fought one of the most "just wars", if for any reasonable men and women there is such a thing, that America had ever been involved in! If Hitler had solidified his domination of Europe and the Japanese had dominated Asia, only God knows what chaos would exist today, if there was going to be a "today" left for the world! Compared to the rest of the world, the lands and cities of America were almost untouched. We even started the MARSHALL PLAN to give aid to Europe, even our enemy, Germany. Russia, who had been our ally during WW2, almost immediately became our enemy because Joseph Stalin was a powerful nitwit who would stop at nothing to solidify his power. Before WW2, during WW2 and after WW2, Stalin was killing or sending 1000's of Russian citizens to prison camps if he thought that, in any way, they were undermining his hold on power. I don't think Stalin worried about whether he was doing the right thing or not! Like Hitler, he was a monster!

Getting back to growing up in Eau Claire I want to mention to the reader some trivia about Eau Claire in the 40's and 50's that, if you or I look at it now, it is not trivia at all. In fact it touches on some of the very issues that exist in our newspapers and TV as I punch these keys on my computer. For a present day 20 year old, or 40 year old or even a 60 year old, certain groups of people might be quite surprised at how life was quite different not too long before they were born. Of course we all know that business and technology have vastly changed. But I am talking about social change! What were your parents views toward race and economic status and education?

Within easy walking distance of my home in Eau Claire was Half Moon Lake. I believe that Half Moon Lake was named that way because it had an almost-island on it called Carson Park. If you could view the water around Carson Park from a helicopter the water would form what looked like a half moon. On the Carson Park land were picnic grounds, a football stadium, practice fields and a very nice baseball stadium for a town the size of Eau Claire. Not only that, but Eau Claire had a farm team of the then Milwaukee Brewers called the Eau Claire Bears. I am telling you this because when I was in the 8th grade one Henry Aaron came to town to play for the Bears. The reason I am telling you this is that you might know that Henry Aaron was a black man! So what, you ask! Well, when I was in the 8th grade I did not know much about racial prejudice. However, prejudice definitely existed in Eau Claire but I did not know about it when Aaron came to town. Only much later did I find out that it was difficult, if not impossible, for Aaron to find any hotel or motel or rooming house that would take him as a guest! I learned much later that the Regis High school coach that coached me as a freshman and sophomore, one Marty Crowe, had reached out to Aaron and let him stay in his home while Aaron played for the Bears. Now, this is not a shocking piece of information now because we all know, or should know, the stories of prejudice regarding Jackie Robinson and the Brooklyn Dodgers or even into the 60's when Vince Lombardi had to dictate that fellow players on the Green Bay Packers would be required to "room together" on road trips without concern for color of skin. The USA was not even close to crossing the bridge to living together in the same house. The odd thing is the fans all loved Aaron because he was a great player, just like they loved Jackie Robinson! But maybe "love" is not the correct word to use here.

The odd part about growing up in a place like Eau Claire is that prejudice never reared it's ugly head until someone sets off the prejudice, like Aaron moving to town. It's not Aaron's fault, of course. If someone at that time had said that Eau Claire was full of prejudice, people would have responded, "what the hell are you talking about!" I was part of the problem but in the 8th grade I was oblivious to the problem. Henry Aaron left town and became one of the greatest hitters in baseball history and Coach Crowe lost his job a few years later but I didn't know until many years later that Henry Aaron lived at Crowe's house!

The prejudice against Jews was also a fact of life in Eau Claire that I was never really aware of until years after I left Eau Claire. When I was in grade school I had a neighborhood friend named Mickey Berman. Our friendship went on in the early grades but when I went to a Catholic High School and he entered Eau Claire High School we quit hanging out together. I believe he was Jewish but, at the time, he and I never talked about it. Also living in Eau Claire were Ann Landers and Abigail Van Buren (not their married names), who both later became quite well known nationally syndicated writers of advice and gossip columns for Chicago newspapers. I guess, in the 8th grade, I didn't know the sisters were Jewish, whatever that meant, but I only knew that Ann drove a white Cadillac convertible and was good looking! What I also didn't know in the 8th grade was that the Nuremberg Trials were going on in Germany to prosecute German judges and military people and Nazis for killing 6,000,000 Jews, Catholics, Protestants, blacks, gays, gypsies, minorities and other citizens of Germany and Europe! It would take a couple more years and more for me to learn that Eau Claire and Milwaukee and Detroit and Atlanta and Birmingham and Moscow and Berlin and the world had a long way to go if they really wanted to prove to themselves that "ALL MEN (and women) ARE CREATED EQUAL!" In fact, in the year 2016, we are still working on that problem across our great Country.

I had two brothers who served in the military, one in the Navy and one in the Army. My dad had served in WW1. I was the youngest in the family and in the fall of 1952 I entered Marquette University in Milwaukee. I also entered the Naval Reserve Officers Training Course as part of my Marquette curriculum. I was about to be thrusted into POLITICS 107! Senator Joseph McCarthy was not only a Marquette graduate but the early 50's were destined to be the apex of his career if anyone saw his career as having an apex! It was also the apex of the cold war, anti-communism, and the House Un-American Activities Committee (HUAC). The Korean War was just starting to wind down which, of course was a civil war ALL ABOUT communism! Even as a freshman at Marquette, I was going to get a lesson in Political Science before taking any political science courses.

It was very popular and most students assumed that it was also patriotic to condemn any person who even smiled when someone said anything positive about the communists, particularly the Russians. For instance, if someone said:

"The Russians lost about 25,000,000 citizens in WW2 fighting for the Allied cause"

That statement might sound to some like you were a "fellow traveler" which was a popular phrase used to describe a person who was "soft on communism", also a popular phrase to this very day. Yes, Stalin was a nasty person and he ruled Russia with an iron hand. He killed many of the 25,000,000 mentioned above. But our own General Schwarzkopf toured Stalingrad with the press in tow a few years back and said that the war in Europe had turned against the Germans when the Russians stopped the Germans at Stalingrad starting in 1942! Now the Stalingrad battle would go on for months in 1942 but the Germans could not push through! Finally, on 02-02-43 surrender came! Field Marshall Paulus along with 22 German generals and almost 100,000 soldiers that had been surrounded gave up the fight. No German Field Marshall had ever surrendered! Hitler believed that Paulus would either fight to the last man or commit suicide. Paulus had answered, "I have no intention of shooting myself for this Bohemian Corporal (Hitler)!"

Back to Marquette University! On TV (a new invention) or in a newsreel, Senator McCarthy would wave packets of papers and yell out to the Press or HUAC or some audience that he had the names of X number of communists right there in his hands! I don't know how many times anyone saw these names aside from Senator McCarthy but it was rare. But between Senator McCarthy and HUAC the careers of 100's of Americans were ruined by "BLACKLISTING" which is basically leaking out that some politician or business person or author or Hollywood writer was "soft on communism!" Many authors and screenwriters had to "ghostwrite" their work and let others put it out because the authors were banned from working! McCarthyism became almost a synonym for anti-communism! Starting in 1947 in the Senate, his career was unremarkable. But in Wheeling, West Virginia on February 9, 1950, speaking to the Republican Women's club, he is quoted to have said:

"I have here in my hand a list of 205---a list of names that were made known to the Secretary of State as being members of the Communist Party and who nevertheless are still working and shaping policy in the State Department."

Within a month after the Wheeling speech, Herbert Block, who signed his cartoons for the Washington Post as "Herblock", coined the name "McCarthyism" in one of his famous drawings and the word would live in history! A million words could be written about McCarthy's decline and demise, but I believe the final blows came in the Army-McCarthy hearings. On June 9th, 1954, Joseph Welch, attorney for the Army suggested that McCarthy turn over the names he said he had for 130 communists or subversives who worked in our defense plants. McCarthy retorted that if Welsh was interested in names of persons aiding the communist party, maybe Welsh should check on a young lawyer in Welsh's own Boston office who had once belonged to the National Lawyers Guild which some suspected of communist leanings. Welch responded:

"Until this moment, Senator, I think I never really gauged your cruelty or your recklessness…(McCarthy tries to repeat his attack but Welch continues) Let us not assassinate this lad further, Senator. You've done enough. Have you no sense of decency, Sir, at long last? Have you left no sense of decency?"

After the Army-McCarthy hearings even some Republican Senators and Congressmen became more vocal and critical of McCarthy's tactics. Then, on December 2nd, 1954 the senate voted 67 to 22 to condemn (considered a censure) Senator McCarthy for his activities. One Biographer said he was a changed man after the censure and became "a pale ghost of his former self." The press and his former senate colleagues, who previously hung on every word McCarthy uttered, now basically ignored him! He died of acute hepatitis and cirrhosis of the liver on May 2, 1957. Most contemporary biographers believe that McCarthy was an alcoholic. He had been in the Senate for 10 years.

If you believe that possibly McCarthy's death might signal a slowdown in attacks on Democrats and Republican "liberals" as communists or "fellow travelers", you would be mistaken. On December 9, 1958, Robert Welsh, (no relation to the Joseph Welsh in the Army-McCarthy hearings) a retired candy manufacturer from New England, inaugurated the JOHN BIRCH SOCIETY. If you thought that McCarthy had made wild and unfair accusations about American citizens being disloyal or commies or worse, please read the following paragraph from Welsh's book about the then current President of the United States:

"On January 20, 1953, Dwight Eisenhower was inaugurated as the thirty-fourth President of the United States. He thus became, automatically and immediately, captain and quarterback of the free-world team, in the fight against Communism. In our firm opinion he had been planted in that position, by Communists, for the purpose of throwing the game.

(Author's note—the above quote is taken from page 133 of Welsh's book titled The POLITICIAN and is copied, underlined & punctuated exactly as in the book.)

I am a Democrat but I have to tell you that I liked President Eisenhower! He was a Kansas boy who became the

Commanding General of ALL ALLIED FORCES-USA—British-French-Canadian-Australian-etc for the invasion of Europe in WW2. He won 2 Presidential terms easily. As he left the Presidency, he warned us of the "Military-Industrial Complex", which he thought of as a money-grabbing collaboration between active or retired Military Officers, politicians and big business in our Country. Even though he was a General of the highest rank and, of course, Commander-in Chief as President, he was a moderate and thoughtful person and I felt I could trust his judgment. Sadly, some in his own party did not!

By the way, if you read more of "The Politician" and you see the 100's of people referred to in that book as being less than loyal to the USA you will be amazed. Senators, Congressmen, UN representatives, journalists, military people, you name your poison. You could come to the conclusion that Welsh was making McCarthy look like a complete amateur in exposing all the purported disloyal citizens in our government, military and in the Press! You might even conclude that Welsh missed McCarthy who had died the year before!

During this period of 1956-1958 I had graduated from Marquette and was commissioned an Ensign in the U. S. Navy. I was assigned to the District Intelligence Office, Ninth Naval District in Chicago, Illinois and worked with both civilian and military personnel doing Security Investigations. Most of these were "background investigations." That meant that if a person in the military or in industry was going to need "secret" or "top secret" clearance to work on some project, the Office of Naval Intelligence (ONI) agents like me would visit his or her College, place of work, etc…to determine if that person was competent and loyal to the United States of America! To dampen your fears that a young person like me would be making these important decisions on loyalty, I will mention that we trained with and worked cases with more veteran investigators. Also, if "problems" did crop up in a given person's background that were troubling, the case would be reviewed by a Security Analyst before they were passed on to higher authority.

Before we leave this Office of Naval Intelligence time in my early life, however, the ONI also investigated GAYS in the military, specifically the Navy, of course. In this 1st chapter I have already mentioned prejudice against blacks, against Jews and now I was learning how deep the prejudice was in this country against Gays! I had already known some Gay references and hate remarks from the high school and college days but it was just "street talk" which didn't qualify as KNOWLEDGE! An investigator would get a tip that a sailor or officer had committed some kind of homosexual act and that person would be brought down to Chicago and given a polygraph test and be interrogated by an agent. These cases were called 6J cases. If the person admitted to doing the deed, so to speak, he or she would be asked to name other Gays in the military and the process would go on. To my knowledge, no one was ever charged with a crime in these instances and I don't believe they were given a dishonorable discharge. But they were discharged with a "General Discharge" and I believe they lost benefits like GI Bill and so on! I was not personally involved in any of these cases during my tenure at ONI. However, much later, when I read serious medical articles and listened to Gay people tell the stories of their life and I realized that Gays were born that way and in 98% of the cases they had no choice in the matter. It was DNA and Hormones calling the shots. I thought, "why are we persecuting them!?" Sometimes people would answer by saying, "if the commies knew that a government worker in the USA was Gay, he could be blackmailed into giving up government secrets in fear of losing his job and his reputation!" My answer is: "NO he couldn't because IF he could tell the Government or the military or his Company that he was Gay then he could NOT be blackmailed!

So we have talked a little about growing up in the Great Depression, Henry Aaron and prejudice, a mention of Jews in my home town, gays in the military, McCarthyism, the Birch Society and Communism. You could almost think of these as 70 year old problems but you would be completely mistaken. There are candidates running for the office of President of the United States in 2016 that call or infer that Barack Obama is a communist or a fascist! They hint that he is a muslim in office to help the muslims defeat America. These are the same thought processes that accused Eisenhower in the 50's of helping the commies! There is still prejudice reported against Jews and blacks and gays each night on our TV's and in our newspapers. We will come back to all that in later chapters.

THE FALSE HOPE OF TRICKLE DOWN ECONOMICS

In President Reagan's first inaugural speech he said the following:

"For decades, we have <u>piled deficit upon deficit</u>, mortgaging our future and our children's future for the temporary convenience of the present. To continue this long trend is to guarantee tremendous social, cultural, political and economic upheavals." (Underlining by author).

Then, 3 paragraphs later he said that words that seem to thrill everyone in the right wing of the Republican Party and especially the conservatives in the Tea Party right to this very minute in 2015!:

"Government is not the solution to our problem; Government <u>is</u> the problem."

People used to brag that President Reagan's philosophy was simple but brilliant and based on a 3—legged stool of beliefs which were 1.) anti-communism, 2.) cut big government and 3.) cut taxes and he started doing that immediately!

Let me make it clear, I am a liberal and a Democrat but I LOVE the ideas put forth in Reagan's 3-legged stool! No wonder so many of the people in the Country supported Reagan! I am an anti-communist because the collectivist societies tend to be nasty warmongers at one extreme or lack empathy for large portions of their society at the other end of their spectrum. However, I don't view all Communist societies as "evil empires" and I don't believe that we are the one and only Judge in the world that decides that these societies should be "realigned" by the USA alone. Vietnam is a good case to look at which we will do later in the book. Secondly, I believe that when conservatives rail against big government they almost always are referring to the social safety net meaning Social Security, Medicare, and now the Affordable Care Act. These are all, of course, programs initiated by democrats over decades to protect the poor and the middle class. I can't tell you the number of times in my life that I have been in a meeting or in a pub and some guy was loudly denouncing social security, as an example. I would ask him: "Are your parents still alive?" "Yes", he would answer. "Do they receive Social Security?" "Yes." "If there were no SS would you be able to support them for the balance of their lifetime?" "No!" So, unlike him I don't want an America where people are walking the street looking for handouts or in dire straits when the local food kitchen is not properly supported. In fact, while I admire the food kitchen people that are trying to help, I would rather live in a Country where food kitchens are not necessary! WE—the USA can be that Country! Thirdly, I like tax cuts just like any man! But when you cut taxes and then can't afford to fund Medicare that I was counting on for 40 years, I might resist your "cutting urge" and suggest that you should not have funded those fighter-bombers that even the Air Force didn't ask you to fund but you funded them anyway because Senator Bigmouth in Texas told his Defense Manufacturer, "don't worry, I'll get it approved!"

The leader of the "cut taxes" group was possibly Arthur Laffer, the reluctant Father of the Laffer curve and "trickle-down economics" in general. The Laffer theory was, basically, the more you cut taxes on millionaires, entrepreneurs and corporations, the higher the Gross Domestic Product will grow and so, even though the <u>tax rates</u> are lower than before, the growth in GDP will make up for that and total <u>tax revenues</u> will increase! As you might know, even George H. W. Bush, who ran against Reagan in the Republican primaries in 1980, called Reagan's economic concepts "voodoo economics!" Then, when Reagan won the election he picked Bush as his VP and Bush had to retreat into a more "silent mode" regarding Reagan's economic and fiscal plans. Bush was correct, by the way, it was "voodoo economics", an outcome apparent to anyone who looked into the results except the right-wing conservative tea-party type Republicans!

At this point I want to give you the definitions of Annual Budget Deficits and Annual Surpluses and then National Debt. The reason I am doing this is because I am convinced that half the politicians, talk show moderators and print journalists are confused themselves or want to confuse the public because their facts are completely wrong when they put them forth!

<u>Budget deficits & budget surpluses--</u> As used in the format of what we are discussing, budget deficits and budget surpluses are based on:

A.) "Annual' calculations. The government decides on an annual budget for a given year--- decides on how much money is needed for the Military--Medicare--- Social Security---Veterans Hospitals---interest on the debt already outstanding---etc. Then, when the fiscal year has passed, we compare what we have spent to the incoming tax $$ the government has collected in taxes from individuals, companies and other sources. If the tax revenues are less than the money spent by the government, that is a yearly budget "deficit". If tax revenues are more than the annual amount spent, it is a budget "surplus" for that year. America has not run many years of budget surpluses but it has been done! I'll get to that later!

B.) <u>NATIONAL DEBT</u> is just adding each year of deficits or surpluses so that we can track the growth over time regarding our total debt since our Country was founded and we started tracking these numbers. If the <u>National Debt</u> was $998,000,000,000 (998 billion) in a given year like 1980 (it was) and the we ran a fiscal deficit of $90,154,000,000 (90 billion) in 1981 (we did), and another deficit of $144,179,000,000 (144 Billion) in 1982 (we did), the <u>National Debt</u> would have grown to $1,232,333,000,000--that is ONE TRILLION & 232 BILLION $! (rnd)

(Please note that numbers are rounded and budgets and calculations are based on Fiscal years—as the government does it, but it is still a year, only the Fiscal year goes from October to September. So when a President takes the oath of office he is already almost 4 months into the fiscal year, a fact that has almost zero bearing on the 8 or 4 year performance of any given President!)

Now that we have absorbed what Reagan said about DEFICIT SPENDING in his 1st inaugural address and clarified how annual deficits and surpluses are accumulated and become added to or subtracted from our National Debt since almost the beginning of our Country, let's see what happened in 1981 to 1993 in the Presidencies of Ronald Reagan and George H. W. Bush:

In the 205 years since 1776 when it all started for America to 1981 which was Carter's last fiscal year, the total NATIONAL DEBT in America had accumulated to $997,855,000,000 (998 billion $$$)!

When President Reagan left office 8 years later the total NATIONAL DEBT had almost <u>tripled</u> to $2,674,636,512,032 (2 TRILLION & 675 BILLION $ (rnd))!

Then, when President George H. W. Bush left office 4 years after Reagan's term expired, the total NATIONAL DEBT had more than <u>quadrupled</u> in the 12 years of Reagan-Bush to $4,136,939,455,492 (4 TRILLION & 137 BILLION $ (rnd)! So, it had taken our Country 205 years to almost reach <u>ONE TRILLION</u> of National Debt but only 12 years later the <u>NATIONAL DEBT WAS 4.14 TRILLION!</u>

Now, if you are a Republican and or a conservative and you are doubting that I am giving you accurate accounts of what actually happened with the budgets in the Presidency of Ronald Reagan, you must read David Stockman's memoir:

<u>The Triumph of Politics, how the Reagan Revolution Failed.</u>

Now, David Stockman was not a Dem like me, no, he was a very conservative Republican Congressman picked by Reagan to be the Director of the Office of Management and Budget, the very job that controls taxes and expenditures for each year that the President is in office! Reagan immediately started in 1981 with substantial tax cuts (Kemp-Roth 1981 tax cuts) that went across the board but favored Corporations and the wealthy because Reagan had become a "supply-sider". Supply-sider are unrelenting in favor of lessening the <u>tax burdens and government regulations</u> so that, theoretically, Gross National Product (GNP—Total goods and services) would grow and then, even though taxes have lower rates, <u>total taxes per year</u> would increase because of those much higher GNP numbers!

By 1983, things weren't looking too good! Annual deficits were way up from the CARTER days and the National Debt was starting to grow at a faster pace! Stockman already had an exercise for the President. Stockman presented 50 "spending categories" to the President and the President could choose a "nick", (a moderate cut) or a whack (a big cut)! "The President enjoyed the quiz immensely", said Stockman, "he sat there day after day with his pencil." But in the end there were too many nicks and not enough whacks! The forecast was that the National Debt would be 800 billion higher over the final 5 years of his Presidency! Stockman suggested that the President should consider a TAX INCREASE! The President pounded his fist on the table! "I don't want to hear any more talk about taxes, the problem is deficit spending!"

Yes, Mr. President, the problem in it's simplest form is in my question as follows: "Are you going to take in enough tax revenues each year to pay for the programs and things you want to spend money on?" Mistakes on either side of that equation will burden the USA with more annual budget deficits and the higher national debt that results. On the expenditures side of the budget, Stockman had frequent confrontations with the Secretary of Defense, Caspar Weinberger. In a big meeting to settle whether the defense buildup should be <u>1.46 TRILLION</u> over 5 years or only <u>1.33 trillion</u>, Weinberger brought 3 cartoon props with him to keep it simple, so to speak!

Number one—A pygmy without a rifle—Representing Jimmy Carter's budget!

Number two--A 4-eyed wimp with a tiny rifle—representing Stockman's budget of 1.33 TRILLION $ (Stockman wore glasses).

Number three—G. I. JOE himself—all decked out in helmet and flak jacket and pointing an M-60 machine gun— representing 1.46 TRILLION!

A reporter later wrote, "Mr. Stockman makes clear that Mr. Weinberger himself had absolutely no idea how to spend all this money at the time he argued it was <u>essential</u> to our national security. He would get as much as he could, then go back to the Pentagon and figure out what to do with it." Stockman left the OMB position in August of 1985. He seemed to know he couldn't stop the inevitable outcome!

Waiting in the wings was an even more conservative player, if that is possible! His name is Bruce Reeves Bartlett. His biography says he is an historian whose expertise is <u>supply side</u> economics—just what we need! Bartlett has worked for half of all the Conservative Groups I have ever heard about (I exaggerate!). He was a domestic policy advisor for Ronald Reagan. He helped draft the Kemp-Roth tax cuts for Reagan. He worked for Ron Paul & the House Banking committee. From 1988 to 1992 he worked for President George H. W. Bush. He worked for the right-wing Cato Institute. Then he worked for 12 years with the National Center for Policy

Analysis in Dallas. In 2005 he criticized George Bush (43) and the National Center fired him! In 2006 he wrote:

"Imposter: How George W. Bush Bankrupted America and Betrayed the Reagan Legacy." In the book he compared Bush 43 to Richard M. Nixon as "two superficially conservative Presidents who enacted liberal programs to buy votes for reelection!" At this point I have to make the following comments which are:

A.) In 2006 Bush 43 had JUST STARTED to bankrupt the Country. In the next 2 years, 2007 and 2008, we were taken in to the greatest recession the Country has seen since the Great Depression. On top of that, friends of the Republicans on Wall Street and some Democrats had conjured up new devices called CREDIT DEFAULT SWAPS which 99% of the people in the financial world didn't seem to understand but they were being pedaled all over the world!

B.) I also have to say that inferring that Bush 43 and Nixon were kind of "liberals in disguise" is a mind-bending idea! While I applaud Bartlett for finally believing the FACTS of the NUMBERS (like 2+2=4), I can't quite squeeze Bush 43 and Nixon into the "liberal camp!"

I am hopeful that Bartlett himself might convert to LIBERALISM and things looked better in 2009 when he said:

"Until conservatives once again hold Republicans to the same standard they hold Democrats, they will have no credibility and deserve no respect. They can start building some by admitting to themselves that Bush caused many of the problems they are protesting."

Then, in 2009, Bartlett wrote: The New American Economy: the Failure of Reaganomics and a New Way Forward, Bartlett said that he:

> "came to the annoying conclusion that Keynes had been 100% right in the 1930's, & that "we needed Keynesian Policies again", and that "no one has been more correct in his analysis and prescription's for the economy's problems than Paul Krugman." Krugman is, by the way, a prominent Nobel-Prize winning liberal economist! <u>Maybe a Bartlett conversion is within reach!</u>

So, what is your point, the reader might ask! Yes, it looks like Reagan might have warned about the bad deficit history of the USA in his 1st inaugural speech and then Reagan, himself, became the <u>deficit champion of the world</u>! The reader might go on to say, President Reagan is dead so what is the point of belaboring this Presidential history? As the author, the *answer is* that since about 1990 to this very day in 2016, all I have heard from 98% of Republicans is that they want current candidates for President, Senator, Congressman, Governor, Mayor, dogcatcher, etc...., whatever the government job might be, the person that holds it should be beholden to the principles espoused by Ronald Reagan---principles that have been shown to be ineffective! **That fact is especially true when applied to the 14 (soon to be less!) Republican candidates running for President in 2016 who state they will emulate the actions of Ronald Reagan when he did great things in the 80's!**

So, dropping off the distrust of communism thing we can mostly agree on, that leaves two remaining legs of the 3-legged stool as espoused by Reagan & Repubs:

1.) Get rid of as many "big government" programs as you can like Obamacare, Medicare, the Voter's Rights Act, Environmental Protection Agency, etc…and rely on the Free Enterprise System to adjust for the inequities of the "market economy". This is the Ayn Rand world where individualism rules. Libertarians call it the <u>Freedom of the Individual!</u> There is NO altruism!

<u>Remember, Government IS the problem!</u>

2.) Above all, cut taxes! The rich WILL benefit but benefits will "trickle-down" to the middle class and the poor! OK, it didn't work in the 80's with supply-side economics but let's try again say the conservative Republicans and the Tea Party. <u>Why</u> do they say that, you ask? Simple! The guys who financed their campaign and hired the lobbyists to approach the candidates are the people who will benefit. Did you notice that Dennis Hastert who was a high school wrestling coach in Illinois before becoming a Congressman and Speaker of the House, then became a lobbyist and a multi-millionaire in just a few short years! There are many success stories to tell about our Senators and Congressmen just like that one! Even Presidential Candidate Donald Trump has affirmed my theory of the lobbyist system in a TV appearance in September of 2015. He intimated that he knows the system backward and forward and he's bought lobbyist influence himself! It works for Trump!

Here is the list of Republican Presidents in the last 100 years that good Conservatives might vote for in the Greatest Republican President contest:

<u>Warren G. Harding</u>—03-04-21 to 08-02-23—Teapot Dome Scandal—other scandals—short timer—Died in office.

<u>Calvin Coolidge</u>—08-02-23 to 03-04-29--For his era, strong on Civil Rights of Blacks and Catholics. However, he set the table for the Great Depression which began only months after he left office.

<u>Herbert Hoover</u>—03-04-29 to 03-04-33--After Woodrow Wilson made Hoover Head of the American Relief Administration after WW1, Hoover organized food shipments to Belgium and other European countries. When he became President in 1929, the Great Depression started 8 months later. By 1932 unemployment was near 25%. 5000 banks had failed. 1000's of Americans congregated in numerous "Hoovervilles" around the Country. What Hoover had done for starvation in Belgium 12 years earlier didn't happen for the Hoovervilles in America!

<u>Dwight Eisenhower</u>—01-20-53 to 01-20-61—I liked him! He ended the Korean war. He was not a fan of Senator McCarthy and not exactly in love with General McArthur. However, as I indicated earlier in this book, the right-wing John Birch Society more than inferred that Eisenhower was disloyal and that is wording it softly! Many other conservative Republicans did, and still do, speak harshly of Eisenhower.

<u>Richard Nixon</u>—01-20-69 to 08-01-74--I'll keep this simple, Nixon was a crook! Listen to the NIXON TAPES! Close

associates of Nixon said that <u>NOTHING</u> went on in the Nixon White House that Nixon did not know about. If that is true, then Nixon was a crook! There were robberies, break-in's, bribes, suppression of evidence, etc…Nixon resigned because he would have been impeached, in which case he would have lost the many perks of a retired President. He wasn't going to miss the payoff.

<u>Gerald Ford</u>— 08-09-74 to 01-20-77—I believe he was a very nice man who came out of the Congress to be VP. Ford was probably the best football player to be President. But he pardoned Nixon and even Republicans didn't rally for him against Carter.

<u>Ronald Reagan</u>—01-20-81 to 01-20-89—As I observed paragraphs ago, 98% of Republicans would say that Ronald Reagan was the greatest Republican President of the last 100 years. I have listed the 8 other republican Presidents so the reader can compare achievements and possibly come to a different conclusion. In Reagan's case, we have already discussed in some detail Reagan's handling of his NUMERO UNO ISSUE, budgets and national debt. As a Democrat, I am not trying to write the history of the Republican party. I don't dislike Ronald Reagan or most of the other Republicans mentioned so far. What I am trying to say is that I am amazed regarding the propaganda that has been dispensed over the years about Reagan's record that is absolutely NOT TRUE! We will explore more of those untruths in upcoming chapters.

<u>George H. W. Bush</u>—01-20-89 to 01-20-93—President Bush only served one term. When he ran for office, he pledged: "read my lips, no new taxes!" What did he DO? He raised taxes! Here is a great irony in the way people look at things. I

thought that decision was a PROFILE IN COURAGE! Why you ask? Because he had always thought that "trickle-down" was voodoo economics and he knew that Reagan had run up far too much national debt. The only way to stop the bleeding was for Bush to raise taxes even though it would jeopardize his reelection!

Please note that I haven't written about George Bush 43 yet in this cavalcade of the 9 Presidents. I will write extensively about him and more about Ronald Reagan in upcoming chapters.

This is not a book about numbers and budgets. That can be boring, but it is necessary and consequential, because I can't just say, "take my word for it."

I have to show you the numbers! Beyond numbers, I want this book to be about the actual history—WHAT really happened. I want it to be about hypocrisy and propaganda. I would like to shed some light on how conservative Republicans hijacked the Republican party over the last 30 years and took Reagan's "government IS the problem" quote and made it their life's work!

REAGAN'S WARS AND
CONFESSION OF GUILT

Some readers will believe that this is an anti-Reagan book. It is not. In the last 100 years, if Calvin Coolidge or Herbert Hoover or George H. W. Bush were the absolute favorite President of Republicans and especially the right wing of that party who in 2016 seem to have a choke-hold on all Republican decisions, I would ignore President Reagan and concentrate my writing on that favorite President. But 98% of the Republican candidates and their advisors and their followers, running for office of the President, Senate, Congress, or any elected office make it clear, on almost every occasion, that the Man from the past that should be emulated by Republicans is President Ronald Reagan. On Meet the Press or Stephanopoulos or Fox news they will have Republican "strategists" and candidates, of course, who say things like "Reagan balanced the budget" or "cut the national debt" and many related claims. Not only did Reagan and Bush (41) not stop huge deficits from accruing but in 12 years in office they ran up the largest national debt % increase in the last 100 years except for the Great Depression—WW2 era and that debt got paid off fast partly because Democrat Truman and Republican Eisenhower had high tax rates on the rich. So, now that we have covered the issue that is most propagandized by the Republican party to this very day, let's move on to the other significant events of history in the Reagan years.

Peace for Galilee

Let's start early in the Reagan presidency. On June 6th, 1982 Israel invaded Lebanon in an operation called "Peace for Galilee." Lebanon was in a civil war between Iran-backed Hezbollah muslims who were supported by the Palestinian Liberation Organization (PLO) and the Syrian forces against Maronite Christian Lebanese forces backed by Israel and the USA. A multinational force came to Beruit 2 months later, officially not to fight but to oversee the evacuation of the PLO guerillas which had been agreed upon by negotiation. The MNF was to keep the peace and consisted of 400 French troops, 800 Italians and 800 Marines of the 32nd Marine Amphibious Unit (MAU).

The USA was there because we supported the new Lebanese President Bachir Gemayel elected on August 23, 1982. We were also there to support Christians in Lebanon and the Israeli army but those goals were not the publicly stated goals. We were there to keep the peace and "oversee" the PLO pullout of their fighters. On 10 September, 1982, the PLO did pull their forces out of Beirut. However, 21 days after being elected, President Gemayel was assassinated. One week later his brother, Amine Gemayel, was made President. Even though the PLO had moved out and buffer zones had been established, the fighting continued.

The worst was yet to come. On 10-23-83 a Mercedes truck carrying a bomb drove through the concertina wire and easily passed from the parking lot into the barracks housing a replacement Marine Detachment, the U. S. 24th Marine Amphibious Detachment (MAU). 241 servicemen were killed—220 marines—18 sailors—3 army soldiers. Another 128 servicemen were wounded, some seriously. Some sources say that this was the worst single day death toll for the American military since the horrific battle of Iwo Jima in WW2! Others say that the Korean War had one day that was worse. Vietnam had never seen that bad of a day. Just minutes later in another part of Beirut, a 2nd truck bomb hit the French Barracks and killed 58 French soldiers, 5 Lebanese and injured many more.

It was learned later that the American National Security Agency (NSA) had learned on September 26, 1983 that Iran had sent to their Ambassador in Damascus, who was calling the shots to Muslim terrorists in Beirut, to "take spectacular action against the American Marines in Beirut!" U. S. Intelligence had intercepted this message but the message was NOT passed on to the Marine Command in Beirut until October 26th or one month after the message was intercepted and 3 days after the BOMBING!

The next disturbing thing learned later was that the Marine Sentries guarding the barracks were ordered to keep their weapons at CONDITION FOUR (no magazine inserted and no rounds in the chamber). Only one sentry, Lance Corporal Eddie Defranco, had time to load and chamber a round but the bomb-truck had already hit the barracks.

The Marine Commander of the 24th MAU, Colonel Timothy Geraghty, deployed as peacekeepers in Beirut, stated that the Americans and French were targeted primarily because of "who we were and what we represented and that it is noteworthy that the United States provided direct naval gunfire support—which I strongly opposed for a week—to the Lebanese Army at a mountain village called Suq-al-Garb on 19 September and the French conducted an air strike on 23 September in the Bekka Valley. American support removed any lingering doubts of our neutrality and I stated to my staff at the time that we were going to pay in blood for this decision."

In his memoir, General Colin Powell, assigned by President Reagan at that time as an assistant to the Secretary of Defense, Caspar Weinberger, sided with Geraghty that, "when the shells starting falling on the Shites (Lebanese muslims), they assumed the 'American Referee' had taken sides."

OPERATION URGENT FURY

If you remember that I mentioned in the first chapter of this book that my home town of Eau Claire, Wisconsin had a population of about 48000 people when I was growing up, the Country of Grenada in the Caribbean had a population of 91000 people when we invaded them in 1983, 2 days after the Marine barracks bombing in Beirut. Grenada had been governed by Great Britain until 1974 when they were granted independence. Why did the USA do this you ask? Because the Reagan Administration sensed a touch of communism creeping into Grenada was the answer. In March of 1983 the President issued warnings about the threat posed to the United States and Caribbean countries by the "Soviet-Cuban militarization" of the Caribbean because of the excessively long runway being built in Grenada. Reagan indicated that the 9000 foot runway and the numerous fuel storage tanks were unnecessary for commercial flights and that evidence indicated the airport was to become a Cuban-soviet forward military base.

Actually, planning of the airport and it's size and location was first proposed by the British in 1954. It was designed by Canadians and partially built by a London firm. Cuban, Libyian, Algerian and contractors of other nationalities had been brought in to work while Grenada was still a British colony. This practice was similar to decades before when the USA needed workers and imported them to build the Panama Canal. In a Country of 91000 people there are often not enough people with the skills and training to design and construct an airport. However, there were Cuban workers in Grenada, they were mostly communists because Fidel Castro said so, and some Caribbean people were worried that that might change the situation with a shaky Grenadian government.

In the invasion of 10-25-83, approximately 8000 soldiers, sailors, airmen and marines took part in OPERATION URGENT FURY and the invasion of Grenada along with 353 "allied" soldiers from 4 or 5 Caribbean and central American countries. All of this was backed up by an armada led by the aircraft carrier Independence and it's battle group of more than 10 ships and related fighter squadrons and helicopter attack squadrons. In all:

—19 American soldiers were killed—45 Grenadians were killed—25 Cubans were killed—24 civilians were killed—18 of those were killed when a mental hospital was mistakenly bombed.

There was a medical school on Grenada that was being attended by a number of American students. It was a carryover from British rule. Besides the "airport reason" for the invasion, the "2nd justification" for the invasion was the "saving of lives" of American medical students before they were mistreated or killed in some communist uprising in the future. I was a loyal watcher at that time of "Nightline" with Ted Koppel which was very big in 1983. I saw his show on the night of the first day of fighting, about 14 to 16 hours of fighting had taken place. He actually called them on the phone during his show at the Medical school and they stated that they were safe and did not feel their lives were in any danger. Then, the next night Koppel called again and the students were in the presence of Army Rangers and said that they were grateful that they were safe. The State Department had already assured them that they could finish med school in the USA.

The international reaction to the invasion was that the United Nations General Assembly adopted resolution 38/7, stating as follows:

"The General Assembly deeply deplores the armed intervention in Grenada, which constitutes a flagrant violation of International law and of the independence, sovereignty and territorial integrity of that state"

The vote was 108 to 9 with only a few island nations and Israel siding with the United States. Everyone else opposed the USA including Canada and Britain with strong words from Prime Minister Margaret Thatcher. The U. S. State Department falsely claimed that a mass grave had been discovered that held the bodies of 100 Grenadians that had been killed by "communist forces."

When Larry Speakes, President Reagan's press secretary, wrote his book, "Speaking Out", in 1988, the chapter that covered the details of the Grenada War was called THE GRENADA FIASCO! It had been ill-planned and ill-advised. It was a cover-up for the bad press that was coming from the Barracks in Beirut! But the Republicans downplayed the word "fiasco" with the phrase "Urgent Fury!". Sounds great, doesn't it, Americans?! *Ironically, the biggest fiasco was yet to come!*

IRAN-CONTRA (ARMS FOR HOSTAGES)

In this chapter we have reviewed the events of **PEACE FOR GALILEE & OPERATION URGENT FURY.** If anything in those 2 stories gave you pause to rethink the history of the Reagan years, get ready to be shocked by **IRAN -CONTRA.**

Before we start, I want to get current for just a moment and mention some recent happenings. Just weeks ago the

Iranian Nuclear Deal was approved by President Obama and, just prior to that, the Prime Minister of Israel came to the USA to address the Congress. He wanted to tell the Congress that Iran was evil and could never be trusted. He might be right and the words I am writing about Iran-Contra, Israel and Arms for Hostages are not critical of Israel or the Israeli government. What my words will show is the *crazy-complexity* of this event and how badly it convolutes the promise by most nations, including the USA, that we will *never negotiate with terrorists or pay for the release of hostages!* In fact, the USA policy was even harsher, namely, *"no negotiations-no concessions."*

The FACTS are that we negotiated for years with Iran and their Lebanon-Syrian proxy, Hezbollah. Worse yet, the reasons the negotiations were so complex was that the negotiations were set up not only to pay for hostage release but to arm our enemy, Iran, and arm the Contras in Nicaragua at the same time without seeming to spend any American tax dollars. Funding of the Contras was illegal because of the passage by the Congress of the Boland Amendment, a name given to 3 U.S. Legislative Amendments between 1982 and 1984. To get around that law, here were the secret steps taken by the Reagan Administration without the knowledge of Congress:

1.) Israel would ship powerful American-made weapons, supplied by the USA to their enemy Iran at a high markup price and get payment. (Remember, Iran was at war with Iraq at this time and needed help!)
2.) The USA would resupply Israel with those weapons and others and Israel would pay the USA.
3.) Colonel Oliver North and many other Reagan aides had worked it out that a portion of the money coming back to the USA would be diverted to fund the Contras in their fight to overthrow the government of Nicaragua

without any accounting by the Congress because the funds were invisible!

As far as we know, the operation went on from 1983 to at least 1986 when a Lebanese magazine publicly reported a weapons for hostages deal. In November of 1986, an airlift of guns were downed in Nicaragua. Eugene Hasenfus, who was captured by the Nicaraguans, said in a press conference that two of his coworkers were with the CIA. That information traveled fast but the whole story would take months to unfold. It was discovered later that immediately after the plane incident, Oliver North and his secretary, Fawn Hall, began shredding evidence of the transactions.

That same November month in 1986, President Reagan appeared on television and stated that the weapons transfers had indeed occurred, but the United States did not trade arms-for-hostages. However, a noted terrorism expert, Magnus Ranstorp from Sweden who studied Hezbollah activities wrote: "U. S. willingness to engage in concessions with Iran and the Hezbollah not only signaled to it's adversaries that hostage-taking was an extremely useful instrument in extracting political and financial concessions from the West but also undermined any credibility of U. S. criticism of other state's deviation from the principles of no-negotiation and no-concession to terrorists and their demands."

Of the American hostages held by Hezbollah and others, Benjamin Weir was released in September of 1985. Terry Anderson, Thomas Sutherland and Terry Waite were released in 1991, long after the arms deal and 3 years after Reagan had left office. Other hostages escaped and others were killed. Remember, at this time, Hezbollah had captive citizens of other nationalities, even the Russians.

At the height of the Iran-contra scandal, I believe that it was Nancy Reagan that saved the Ronald Reagan presidency. On November 13, 1986, still in strong denial, President Reagan went on television and said:

> "in spite of wildly speculative and false stories of arms for hostages and alleged ransom payments, we did not, repeat, did not, trade weapons or anything else for hostages, nor will we." (A Nixonian type of lie but worse).

Then very strange things began to happen! Robert Strauss had once been the the Chairman of the Democratic party, but was a switch-hitter and had worked for Republicans from time to time. The Reagans liked him. Sometime after the above statement by Reagan, a call went out from Nancy Reagan to Robert Strauss to come over to the White House and have a one-on-one talk with the President about the possibility of impeachment. We do not know whether Strauss used the word *impeachment* when he met with Reagan, what we do know that it was being used by many people in the Congress and in the Press.

"I told the President the truth", Strauss recalled, "and advised Reagan to dismiss all the aides who had touched the scandal." According to both Nancy Reagan and Strauss, the President was quite irritated with the conversation. But Nancy Reagan called Strauss later that night and told him: "that was very brave tonight…it was something that needed to be done and had to be done…he (the President) heard every word you said, and I know Ronnie, and in the next day or two, he'll get rid of Don Regan (Chief of Staff) which is what he has to do!"

As you can tell from Mrs. Reagan's writings, she was not a fan of Donald Regan. It was commonly said that Regan made decisions without consulting the President and Nancy seemed to feel he was grabbing too much power. Donald Regan wrote in his memoir: "On February 23, 1987, the Monday before the release of the Tower Board's Report (on Iran-Contra & who-did what), the President and I had agreed, in the painful conversation in the oval office that I have described, that I would resign as Chief of Staff soon after the Tower Report was issued. No specific date or time for my departure was discussed."

The President decided to speak to the nation about the Tower Board's findings on Iran-Contra, hold a press conference and deliver a major foreign-policy speech, all in March 1987. It was at this point that I believe that Nancy Reagan decided to step into the vacuum and guide her Husband to the finish line. Here were the big obstacles to jump in the last 2 years of the Reagan presidency!

1.) She had already orchestrated bringing in Bob Strauss who had suggested a big "housecleaning" starting with Chief of Staff Donald Regan but she already knew there would be many more.

2.) Mrs. Reagan knew that the President could end his Presidency by Impeachment and she did not seem to trust many of the President's aides to guide him through these final 2 years.

3.) Mrs. Reagan was wise enough to know that another meeting with Mikhail Gorbachev would be in the future and a great success there might make all of America forget Iran-Contra.

4.) There is another possible hurdle that had to be overcome but it is just guess-work on my part. Mrs. Reagan might have sensed that President Reagan was having "memory problems" at some point in this timeline. Compared to today, little was known about Alzheimers at that time but what if she sensed it early on but with time still left in his Presidency. What we know now is that Mr. Reagan was in "early Alzheimers." There were rumors that the President could not remember the names of some of his aides in the White House at different times. Reagans son, Ron Reagan, wrote in the book titled, <u>My Father at 100</u>,: "Three years into his first term as President...I was feeling the first shivers of concern that something beyond mellowing was affecting my Father." Watching the 1984 Reagan-Mondale debate he writes: "I began to experience the nausea of a bad dream coming true. My heart sank as he floundered his way through his responses, fumbling with his notes, uncharacteristically lost for words. He looked tired and bewildered."

If this were true, what would you do if you were the wife of the President? Would you tell him he has this problem which he probably wouldn't believe and risk his alienation? If he believed you, should he retire for the good of the Country? Or would you and the President ride out the next two years and try to beat Impeachment and end with a great success negotiating with Gorbachev? In any event, there is no shame in having Altzheimers!

The one thing that you can't ignore is the unlimited drive that Mrs. Reagan had to control events in the White House. A memoir written by Don Regan stated: "Virtually every major move and decision the Reagans made during my time as White House Chief of Staff was cleared in advance with a woman in San Francisco (an astrologer from San Francisco named Quigley) who drew up horoscopes to make certain that the planets were in favorable alignment for the enterprise." No matter what you think of Regan, other sources supported these horoscope comments. The President decided he was going to speak to the nation about Iran-Contra, have a press conference and and deliver a foreign policy speech, all in March 1987. So the word went out to the astrologer to guide them toward the best dates for the President to schedule the above speeches and press conference. Ms. Quigley came back with the following advice according to Regan:

Late Dec thru March bad—Jan 16-23-very bad—Jan 20 nothing outside WH possible attempt—Feb 20-26 be careful—March 7-14 bad period—March 10 to 14 no outside activity—March 16-very bad—March 21 no— March 27 no—March 12 to 19 no trips exposure—March 19 to 25 no public exposure—April 3 careful—April 11 careful—April 17 careful—April 21 to 28 stay home.

None of this is really funny but I just have to say that Ms. Quigley was definitely not a starry-eyed optimist! With this kind of advice you would have to hole up in a cave somewhere! But both the Reagans relying on her advice does show that Mrs. Reagan had a **heavy influence** on what would happen in the White House and in the Country in 1987 and 1988. President Reagan relied on his wife and especially now when more people were going to be fired, indicted and pointing fingers at each other! It would be a tumultuous and unpredictable 1987 and 1988! Just before Christmas in 1986, the Los Angeles Times had written (Jack Nelson): "Deaver and Spencer, (key Reagan advisors) supported by First Lady Nancy Reagan, plan to advise Reagan that his Presidency will be seriously hampered during his final 2 years unless he ousts Regan and takes other strong steps to address the Iranian arms-and-hostages scandal." In the end, there were many people high up in the White House involved. Here is the scorecard:

- William Casey, CIA Director, stricken hours before he was to testify, died.
- Caspar Weinberger, Secretary of Defense, pardoned by Bush (41) before trial.
- Oliver North, NSC operative, convicted but conviction overturned.
- Robert McFarlane, convicted, later pardoned by President George Bush.
- Elliott Abrams, Asst. Sec of State, plea bargain, 2 yrs. Probation, pardoned.
- Alan Fiers, Chief CIA, central America, 1 year probation, pardoned by Bush.
- Clair George, Covert Ops-CIA, pardoned by Bush before sentencing.
- Fawn Hall, North's secretary, given immunity from prosecution for testimony.
- John Poindexter, convicted of perjury & obstruction, Court overturned.
- Jonathan Scott Royster, Liason to Oliver North, pardoned before trial by Bush.
- Duane Clarridge, CIA senior official, 7 counts of perjury, pardoned by Bush.

The above legal shenanigans lasted well into the Bush years. No one served any time. But back on March 3, 1987, the President went on TV and said the following:

"A few months ago I told the American people I did not trade arms for hostages. My heart and my best intentions still tell me that's true, but the facts and the evidence tell me it is not. As the Tower board reported, what began as a strategic opening to Iran deteriorated, in it's implementation, into trading arms for hostages. This runs counter to my own beliefs, to administration policy and to the original strategy we had in mind."

(As an author's note to what President Reagan said above, I am a firm believer in "facts and evidence!" **THAT is why I am writing this book!** But even the above statement is not "the truth—the whole truth—and nothing but the truth!" Note that he admits the trading-for-hostages part of the transactions, but says NOTHING about shipping arms to Nicaragua. IF—if he admitted that it would involve him illegally violating the Boland Amendment, a potentially impeachable offence. Remember, Reagan made this statement prior to all the indictments and court proceedings listed above which actually took place in the 1987 to 1991 period.)

Sometime after Reagan made the above "confession statement", Oliver North stated: "Ronald Reagan knew of and approved a great deal of what went on with both the Iranian initiative and private efforts on behalf of the Contras and he received regular, detailed briefings on both... I have no doubt that he was told about the use of residuals (invisible money) for the Contras and he approved it."

Let me say this about Colonel Oliver North. He seems to be everything a person should be as a U. S. Marine Officer. If his boss, Admiral Poindexter, who worked under the Secretary of Defense, who, in turn, worked for the President of the United States, was asked to deliver arms to the Contras in Nicaragua and evidently Poindexter picked North to do the job. It is NOT up to North to decide whether the President had violated the Boland Amendment. North was following orders!

Reagan-Gorbachev Meetings

President Reagan and General Secretary Gorbachev were destined to meet 3 times while they were both in office. Before talking about those meetings, let's review a short biography of each leader that possibly will shed some light on how their negotiations ended and what was accomplished.

President Ronald Reagan

Ronald Reagan was born in Tampico, Illinois on February 6, 1911. In 1932 he graduated from Eureka College in Illinois with a major in Economics. In 1935 he enlisted in the Army Reserves. In 1940 he married actress Jane Wyman. In 1941 daughter Maureen was born. In 1942 he was called to active service but was not allowed in combat because of eyesight problems. He is then transfered to the Army Air Corps to make training films. In 1945 he adopts a son, Michael, and is discharged from the Army.

With the above basics out of the way we start to see the early political changes. In 1947 he becomes President of the Screen Actor's Guild which makes him a union leader. He is acknowledged as a Democrat. He divorces Wyman and in 1949 marries Nancy Davis. In 1954 Reagan became Host of the General Electric Theater. He was a "different" Democrat and voted for Eisenhower and supported Nixon in the 1960 Kennedy victory. He registers as a Republican in 1962. In 1964 he becomes a national figure with his "A Time for Choosing" speech for Barry Goldwater.

I had personal friends that were in early management jobs at GE in the 60's. I believe that Reagan became a Conservative in the early 50's, if not before, and that his spokesman's job with GE was pivotal in that change. This did not mean that all of GE was conservative in politics, so to speak, but it was the nature of the job and how his persona melded into the high level business community. Reagan streamlined a message of patriotism—free enterprise—business is good—Government is bad—taxes are bad—regulations are bad—Russia is an evil empire—Communists are bad whether they are in Iran, or Grenada, or Nicaragua, or Vietnam. We, the USA, have an obligation to wipe out the commies. He didn't say all this in each GE speech but over the years the speech could morph into any of the above points.

Reagan was invited to speak in many venues and you could almost say that speeches were his profession. A Political Science professor from UC-Berkeley published a series of papers making a case that Reagan's thinking was profoundly influenced by the movies he had been in or viewed. Speaking to the Congressional Medal of Honor Society in 1983 when he was President, he told a WW2 story of a B-17 Captain whose plane had been hit and was unable to drag his wounded young, ball-turret gunner out of the turret. Instead of parachuting to safety with the rest of the crew, the Captain took the frightened boy's hand and said, "never mind, Son, we'll ride it down together." The problem was that no such Captain existed. The story came from a 1946 movie, "A Wing and a Prayer."

Within a month of that telling that story in 1983, Reagan told Israeli Prime Minister Yitzhak Shamir that the roots of his concern for Israel could be traced back to WW2, when he, as a signal corps photographer, had filmed the horrors of Nazi death camps. Reagan, however, never left the USA during WW2. He apparently had seen a documentary about the camps.

So, thru the GE years, then as Governor and as President, his goals were in support of big business and less taxes on business and distrust of government. Here is one of Reagan's famous quotes:

"The best minds are not in Government, if any were, business would hire them away."

So, along with anti-communism, the tripod of the legs of the stool mentioned in Chapter 2 are in place and growing. By the way, Reagan was correct in many ways. Many people have left Congress & related influential government jobs and are now lobbyists making huge money, paid by large corporations, making back-room deals to stop movements like—the anti-smoking movement in the 60's—clean water and the EPA in the 70's—acid rain protestations—anti-HIV research in the 80's—Global warming and the Carbon tax. A famous book has been written to document these efforts but the beat goes on to this very moment! We will discuss these matters in a future chapter of this book.

General Secretary Mikhail Gorbachev

Mikhail Gorbachev was born on March 2, 1931 in Privolnoye, Soviet Union, in a mixed Russian-Ukrainian family. He is, therefore, 3 years older than me which is not important, but I had to mention it anyway. As a child he survived a famine in 1933 that killed nearly half the population of his village. His Father was a WW2 vereran. Mikhail graduated from Moscow State University in 1955 with a degree in law. While at the University he joined the communist party of the Soviet Union.

Gorbachev worked his way up through the party. In 1972, he headed a soviet delegation to Belgium and in 1975 another delegation to West Germany. In 1983 he visited Prime Minister Trudeau in Canada. Then in 1984 he went to Great Britain and met with Prime Minister Margaret Thatcher. She thought he could be easy to work with. These trips signaled that his power in the Soviet Union was growing. Then General Secretary Andropov died in 1984 and his replacement, Chernenko, died a year later. On March 11, 1985, Gorbachev was elected General Secretary. He was also, at 54, the youngest General Secretary and the first GS to be born after the Russian revolution of 1917.

In the 27th Congress, Gorbachev's goal was to change the party and the economy with concepts of GLASNOST (openness), PERESTROIKA (restructuring), USKORENIYE (acceleration of economic development) and DEMOKRATIZATSIYA (democratization).

In Gorbachev's own words, Perestroika was the "conference of the development of democracy, socialist self-government, encouragement of initiative and creative endeavor, improved order and discipline, MORE glasnost, criticism and self-criticism in all spheres of our society. It is utmost respect for the individual and consideration for personal dignity."

On April 8th, 1985, six months before meeting President Reagan for the first time in Geneva, Gorbachev announced the suspension of the deployment of SS-20's in Europe as a starter to resolving intermediate-range nuclear weapons issues.

The Geneva Summit

Reagan and Gorbachev met in Geneva, Switzerland on November 19, 1985. They had amiable meetings and seemed to respect each other. The two had made some agreements on lower level issues. Donald Regan, Chief of Staff, summarized the meetings this way: "the outcome of the Geneva Summit was even more favorable than I imagined it would be…all these were worthy achievements, but ambassadors working in obscurity could have made them come to pass. What really mattered were the intangibles. Reagan and Gorbachev had discovered that they could talk to each other, even if they could not yet agree." Regan already knew that they disagreed on President Reagan's Strategic Defense Initiative.

The Reykjavik Summit

It was the last day. Reagan and Gorbachev had spent almost an hour strolling the grounds, hammering out the final points of conflict with only their interpreters present, which was out of the ordinary because no staff members, like Don Regan, could monitor the give and take. Now the two groups of negotiators were putting words down on paper. (The following is related from Don Regan's book, For the Record.) As they waited for staff to complete paperwork, Reagan asked Gorbachev, "what had he meant in an earlier letter referring to the 'elimination of all strategic forces'?" Gorbachev had responded: "I meant I would favor the elimination of *all nuclear weapons,*" was Gorbachev's answer!

*"All n*uclear weapons", Reagan said. "Well, Mikhail, that's exactly what I have been talking about all along. That's what we have long wanted to do—get rid of all nuclear weapons. That's always been my goal." "Then why don't we agree on it?" Gorbachev asked. "We should, Reagan said, that's what I've been trying to tell you." Then came the impasse. Gorbachev said, "I agree, but this must be done in conjunction with

a 10 year extension of the ABM treaty and a ban on the development and testing of SDI outside the laboratory."

According to Regan, that was the ballgame! Regan wrote, "Reagan, astonished by this sudden reversal, said, absolutely not. I am willing to discuss all details, including the timing, of a plan to eliminate all nuclear weapons in conjunction with a plan to reduce conventional forces to a state of balance. But I will not discuss anything that gives you the upper hand by eliminating SDI."

The meeting was over. Depression was in the air. Evidently what had just been said about SDI came up in in one of the earlier talks at Reykjavik. On the way to the airport Regan said that the President repeated the word *laboratory* over and over. Then the President said to Regan: "It even got to a personal level, Don. I said to Gorbachev, I think we've developed a good relationship. I'm asking you personally to give me this. You've got your ten years, (extension of ABM); I understand why you need it. But I promised the American people that I wouldn't trade away their future security, which is SDI. But Gorbachev wouldn't give in, even to my personal plea."

Regan had called his forces together before leaving for the airport. They included Pat Buchanan, David Chew, Dennis Thomas, Tom Dawson and Larry Speakes, who was the press secretary. "Look, were going to have to put a speech together for the President at Keflavik (name of airport) that reflects some of what happened today but doesn't reflect any kind of defeat. Let's work fast."

Washington Summit

In December of 1987, President Reagan and GS Gorbachev met for the 3rd and last time while they were both in office. They signed an Intermediate Range Treaty (INF) to eliminate

4% of each of the superpowers nuclear arsenals. It allowed for onsite monitoring of the weapons by both sides. It was a good start and I am happy that President Reagan stayed in the negotiations despite the fact that he didn't get his coveted SDI which he had pushed for in the first two meetings.

The reader should note that today in 2015, 28 years after the Reagan-Gorbachev meetings, we still don't have the SDI system, at least that we know about. I said 28 years, but it is 48 years since 1967 when Edwin Teller (Father of the H-bomb), spoke about SDI in a lecture at Lawrence Livermore Laboratories in California! Many Generals, Scientists, Politicians and Economists called SDI, *Starwars*, because the implementation of it was so complex and expensive and because it called for satellites in space shooting down every nuclear missile shot from anywhere on the planet.

I would like to ask the reader this question: Gorbachev said to Reagan at Reykjavik, "I would favor the elimination of all nuclear weapons." Reagan answered: "Well, Mikhail, that's what I have been talking about all along…that's always been my goal." My question is: *wouldn't it have been smart of Reagan to* eliminate all nuclear weapons, *which they both said they wanted, even if he or Gorbachev would not get to develop SDI?"*

While we are speaking of the summit at Reykjavik, let me jump to 2015 and the evolving theme of this book, which is the 97% of Republicans that would emulate the policies of Ronald Reagan if they were to become President or attain a high office.

In July of 2015 in a TV ad, Chris Christie said: "President Obama gave away the store to the Iranians…you would not let this President buy a car for you at a car dealership. I would have walked away from the table. That's what Ronald Reagan did when he walked away from Mikhail Gorbachev in Reyakjavik."

Then, Carly Fiorina, in a Republican Debate, said that she would not negotiate with Putin if she were President. Recalling the wisdom of Reagan she said, "Ronald Reagan walked away at Reykjavik."

Sorry, Christie and Fiorina, but saying to Gorbachev after he rejected SDI, "I'm asking you *personally* to give me this (SDI), but Gorbachev wouldn't give in, even to my personal plea," is not exactly walking away, especially when Reagan could have said, "OK, **all** nuclear weapons!"

After the Washington summit and into 1988, the dominoes started to tumble in the Iran-Contra saga. North and Poindexter were indicted on March 16, 1988. The White House was on edge all the way to January 20, 1989 when President George H. W. Bush was sworn in as the 41st President. Even democrats did not have the heart to pursue another Watergate type of period in history.

Gorbachev's abandonment of the restraints of the Brezhnev Doctrine allowed upheavals in eastern Europe satellite countries. The loosening of Soviet controls across Europe ended the cold war. For his Perestroika goals, Gorbachev was awarded the German Otto Hahn Peace Medal in 1989 and on 15 October 1990 Gorbachev was awarded the Nobel Peace Prize in Oslo. It's a shame that all Russians didn't approve of Gorbachev's actions because he was basically forced out of office on 27 December 1991. Boris Yeltsin moved in. Putin was still young but must have been apoplectic over Gorbachev's loosening of Soviet controls over eastern Europe. Would the world fall back again into hostility in the 21st century?

RIGHT WING RADIO &
TV GRAB THE BATON

Before Reagan left office in early 1989, in 1987 he left a present on the table for the man who would become the most powerful conservative republican in the nation for at least the next 20 years, if not right to this present day. That man was Rush Limbaugh and the present Reagan left him was the repeal of the Fairness Doctrine which, prior to that time the FCC had required that radio stations provide free air time for responses to any controversial opinions that had been aired by the station. The Wall Street Journal, by no measure a liberal newspaper, wrote an editorial that said, "Ronald Reagan tore down this wall (the Fairness Doctrine) in 1987…and Rush Limbaugh was the first man to proclaim himself liberated from the East Germany of liberal media domination." I am not the first person to express an opinion that Limbaugh was an important power broker. Many Republicans were fearful of disagreeing publicly with Limbaugh and were especially reluctant to "call him out" on issues because they knew that he could destroy them with his "radio bully pulpit" where the insults fell like rain whether they were accurate or not.

Why did I come to believe that Limbaugh was so powerful a voice for the Republican right wing? In the late 1990's thru the early 2000's, I drove from my home in Missouri up to a cottage in Northern Wisconsin on a frequent basis. While I was in the Wisconsin northwoods, I would go into a bar or café in some little town and the local contractors and shop workers would be there having a "Limbaugh lunch", meaning Rush would be broadcast in the bar or café thru the noon hour and beyond and it was apparent that was how the locals got much of their "news". But thinking this was a rural, small town experience would be a serious error. This became apparent on my 600 mile trip back to Missouri. Wausau would have Rush on the radio—then WLS in Chicago—then KMOX in St. Louis. These stations were the *Radio Heavies!* The other shocking part of the experience was that the radio stations involved undoubtedly understood that they had a conservative Limbaugh audience listening in so they hired more conservatives to have shows following Limbaugh. Sometimes it would be 8 or 9 hours of conservative talk on my drive up or back. In the 90's, the constant attacks on President Clinton and Hillary were relentless but all liberals were targeted and the insults are still coming to this day.

This meant, over the days and weeks and months and years of broadcasting in the 1990's and beyond, millions of radio listeners in Wisconsin and across the Country were being schooled by Limbaugh and learning the lessons that he taught about politics and the deficiencies of democrats—liberals—the National Press—President Clinton—President Obama—Nancy Pelosi—Harry Reid—Barbara Streisand—and a list of similar people and institutions that has no end! That strategy, by the way, is a proven winner for hate-mongers. People who look at long lists of people or institutions denigrated by a person like Limbaugh, say to themselves, "gee, I like Barbara Streisand but I don't like that Nancy person. Maybe Rush makes some sense here!"

I have two old friends, Up North, as the saying goes, who both had sons that listened to Rush in their car radios in their early work lives in the 90's. Both of the sons were not too long out of high school and to my knowledge were "nonpolitical in their early years." However, they spent hours each day in their car or truck and many listening hours with Limbaugh. Eventually, they were taping the radio shows and sending the tapes to their parents so they could be informed by Limbaugh also. It became an obsession for the young ones, if not the parents. Evidently, making nasty allegations against politicians or other famous people was going to become the mantra of this *new* talk radio. Guess who were some of the first ones to sign up and begin their own talk show careers? They were both felons—G. Gordon Liddy and Charles Colson! The Nixon "Dirty Tricks" department was going back into business.

It was 1992, Rush Limbaugh was going to the stratosphere of talk radio and you could say almost anything you wanted because of the rescinding of the Fairness Doctrine. Limbaugh was making millions and Gordon Liddy probably surmised that there was *money to be made*! Yes, he was a convicted felon. He had been closely involved with the White House plumbers unit in the Watergate break in of Democratic Headquarters. Most sources believed he had knowledge of the break in at Daniel Ellsberg's psychiatrist's office. People said he would do almost anything to deprecate the people on President Nixon's "enemies list!" He was sentenced to 20 years but, ironically, President Carter commuted Liddy's sentence and he finally only served 52 months. But now, in 1992, he could do what he could not do in the Nixon Dirty tricks office. What is that you ask? He could make accusations and hurt the reputations of the people he opposed by being a radio show host. He was already good at that. Dems-liberals-progressives-President Clinton—there would be many targets. On top of that, he could have a slice of the possible twenty million people out there that were staunch conservative Republicans and could give their allegiance to Liddy as well as Rush without missing a beat!

Chuck Colson was a different talk show host. Along with Liddy, he had been an aggressive Nixon dirty-tricks operative. Then, in 1973, when he knew he would be going to prison for his tricks, he became a Christian. After prison, he founded a *Prison Ministry Fellowship* and built a career on religion and prison reform. In 2008 President George W. Bush awarded Colson the *Presidential Citizens Medal,* one of the highest awards a civilian can be awarded. I don't know if he is the only felon to ever receive that very high award, but I will make a bet there aren't many felon honorees! I did not follow Mr. Colson's career closely after Nixon left office and I realize he may have done some good things. I did, however, see him interviewed several times on TV over the years and he came off as an arrogant, unrepentant person without any contrition about how he had let down the Country and contributed to the trauma of our great Nation! Like Liddy, he started his radio show in the early 90's and his assault on liberals and Democrats lived on.

I mentioned Liddy and Colson but I am not trying to do this chronologically in time. The floodgates were primed and would burst wide open for the next 25 years. Coming down the pipe would be Bill O'Reilly—Sean Hannity—Mike Savage—Alex Jones—Glenn Beck—Mike Gallagher—Laura Ingraham—Neil Boortz—Bill Bennett—Michael Medved—Larry Elder and many more.

In a 1992 letter, Ronald Reagan thanked Limbaugh "for all you are doing to promote Republican and conservative principles…you have become the Number One voice for conservatism in our Country." In 1993, he was inducted into the National Radio Hall of Fame.

To illustrate Limbaugh's *"staying power", a* New York times journalist, Zev Chafets, wrote a book titled "Rush Limbaugh: An Army of One" in 2010 wrote after the 2010 primaries that Limbaugh was "the brains and the spirit behind" the Republican Party's "resurgence" in the wake of the 2008 election of President Barack Obama. Chavets pointed to Senator Arlen Specter's defeat after being labeled by Limbaugh, "Republican in Name Only", with additional plaudits to Sarah Palin, whose big applause line, "Republicans are not just the party of no, but the party of hell, no", came from the repertoire of Mr. Limbaugh.

As we moved to the middle 90's, another conservative icon would appear in a relatively new technology, namely the internet. Matt Drudge had moved to Los Angeles and created the Drudge Report. The news and gossip that he e-mailed to friends morphed into a service to keep abreast of the news of the day and other interesting developments from various news sources and contacts that he developed. Sometimes he would latch on to a rumor of some importance and break an important story ahead of the *mainstream press,* the more gentle name than most conservatives use when they speak of the New York Times or the Washington Post or even small town newspapers who say something nice about a liberal a couple times a year.

Finally, as we rolled into the 2000's and technology was running wild, we entered full bore into the world of cable and satellite TV. Our *news world* was no longer going to be NBC-CBS-ABC-PBS and some small regional and local broadcasters. 100's of TV networks would be in play across the world and the sharing of the "news" cycle would seem to go at warp speed. Most all of these changes, the new popularity of talk radio, the birth of heavy usage of the internet and the satellite technology allowing information to be shared almost at the speed of light around the globe had a profound effect in many areas, especially in print journalism.

Almost from the inception of our Country but especially in the 20th century, newspapers and magazines were almost part of our DNA. The Hearsts and the Pulitzers and many others were an integral part of lives, even if we didn't know them. The news and the editorials and even the sports and cartoons were part of the family tradition in a sense. The reading and sharing of a Sunday newspaper was often a 3 or 4 hour tradition when I was a little younger. The news services like AP and UPI allowed sharing of stories from LA to Poughkeepsie to London and Toyko and allowed smaller town newspapers to share in national and international news.

However, newspapers are expensive businesses to run and keep profitable. In newspapers and in TV, which sometimes share some professional reporters or other sources of news, it is expensive to have your own correspondent staff around the USA and the world. To pay to get that done a publisher needs subscriptions and advertising to pay the bills. That business model is under attack! Newspapers are failing. When I was 20 I read newspapers almost daily. My Grand children that are 20 are not reading newspapers. They are not dumb but it is the way things are. They are spending far more hours per day looking at electronic devices than I did reading newspapers! I pray that what they are looking at on the devices is at least somewhat beneficial!

Now, I am an 81 year old guy but I am not against change. In fact, as I have lived through it for these 81 years I have, for the most part, adjusted to the times and the games being played. But the big question I am raising in this chapter of this book is as follows:

"Where are we, the citizens of the USA and the world, going to be getting our news and our information, right now and in the future, that we need in order to make good judgements in our lives and pass that information onto future generations? Are we going to get that information from the Rush Limbaugh radio show? How about the internet and the Drudge Report? Maybe we should rely on Fox as millions of republicans do? Is the news we are going to get from FOX the truth or *propaganda* of Republicans?"

Let's hear what a powerful Republican strategist said on ABC TV:

FOX NEWS IS THE MOST POWERFUL ORGAN IN THE REPUBLICAN PARTY!

Alex Castellanous------on THIS WEEK----December 31, 2015

So it looks as though the Republicans have the most powerful force in radio (Limbaugh) and also the internet (Drudge) and in TV (Fox)! If you are a conservative and you don't know who Castellanous is, there are many more Republicans who agree with him just like Reagan earlier when he said about Limbaugh, "you have become the Number One voice for conservatism in our Country!" So I will reword my question from above as follows:

"Given that both Ronald Reagan and Alex Castellanous and many other Conservative Republican "talkers" and politicians believe that Limbaugh and Fox and maybe Drudge are reliable organs of the Republican party, is that where you and your family want to get their "news" and information in the future?"

If the answer to the above is YES, then you might have picked the right party and philosophy of life. You probably believe, then, that the so-called National Liberal Media has been poisoning your mind all these years because that is the daily song that is sung by the vast majority of TV and radio "Talkers", as their magazine calls them and as most conservative Republicans politicians also claim.

You then must think that Edward R. Murrow, Walter Cronkite, Chet Huntley, David Brinkley, Howard K. Smith, Tom Brokaw, Charlie Rose, Lester Holt, Richard Engel and scores of other journalists in TV and print that I have not listed were just pawns of the liberal, wicked media! I am not even sure that the people above are liberals or conservatives. I have listened to them and many others over the years and I have never, that I can recall, heard any of them, using nasty words, insult the President of the United States. I never heard them call a young woman "a slut" on the air! I never heard them applaud a Presidential candidate who would say in a televised debate to a sitting President, *we are going to kick your rear end out of the White House.*

One of my favorite Conservative TV shows is the Glenn Beck show. I watch 10 minutes of Beck and O'Reilly and listen to 10 minutes of Limbaugh every few days just to get a feeling what "propaganda stories" are being pushed on behalf of the Republican Party during a given period. You might believe 10 minutes is not enough but I have been doing this for years and at almost ANYTIME that I tune in the subject is the same. It is an attack on Democrats and liberals anywhere in the cosmos! Did you ever notice the effort that is put forth to convince the watcher or listener that the information coming out of the TV or radio is actually true!

Their mottos are: The truth lives here - No political agenda - Hard hitting & fair - Tells the stories the mainstream won't touch - There is no left or right, just right or wrong - The spin stops here - Pinheads (meaning liberals) - We only speak the truth etc... Why is it that both the Blasé(Beck) and Fox find it necessary to have multiple mottos that assure audiences that they don't intend to toss untrue news and/or "facts" at their audiences each day as they start their broadcasts? I don't remember Huntley or Brinkley starting out their show by saying: "we're going to tell you the truth today." That would be weird, wouldn't it?

My favorite conservative motto was months (04-07-15) ago when Beck looked at the camera and proclaimed in a very serious voice:

A NEWS NETWORK CANNOT BE AN ACTIVIST NETWORK! (04-07-15)

It was shocking! I always thought that Beck wanted to be in the "news business." I thought that he wanted to study the happenings around the world and have a TV station that disseminated the "news" to the public in an accurate and truthful way! But if Beck refused to ever run an "activist network", then he couldn't come on the air and proselytize for Ted Cruz for President, as an example, because that is WHAT ACTIVISTS DO! I don't believe Walter Cronkite ever endorsed anyone for President from his network post before the election and Cronkite was accused of being part of the "liberal colossus" as the right wing calls the Press on many occasions. Cronkite didn't want to be an **activist** in journalism! Beck, as I understand it, wants someone to obliterate "OBAMACARE" and he seems to believe that only a conservative Republican will do that job. Also, I don't know if he believes that Ted Cruz is the modern Galileo, like Cruz said he was, but that discussion will be covered in a future chapter of this book. Suffice to say, it seems that most of the presenters on the Blasé are playing the Galileo role with Cruz because they all laugh it up about liberals believing in Global Warming! Is that the non-activist role? I wouldn't think so!

I believe that Beck has said he is a libertarian. In case someone out there reading this book isn't sure what libertarians believe, please let me try to define this title. First of all, libertarians are NOT liberals by any stretch of the imagination. Libertarians believe that Government, particularly the Federal Government, should be severely limited in it's powers. To illustrate how limited they believe the federal government should be, I want to take you back to the Presidential election of 1980 and pick some of goals of the Platform of the Libertarian Party in that election as follows:

- We support the eventual repeal of all taxation.
- We support the abolition of the Environmental Protection Agency.
- We favor the repeal of the Social Security System. Pending that repeal, participation in Social Security shall be made voluntary
- We call for the dissolution of the Department of transportation.
- We urge the repeal of Federal Finance Laws.
- We oppose all government welfare, relief programs & "aid to poor" programs.
- We support abolition of the Department of energy.
- We support abolition of the Food and Drug Administration (FDA).
- We favor the abolition of Medicare and Medicaid programs.
- We support the repeal…of Minimum wage laws.
- We oppose all corporate & personal income taxation, including capital gains.

I could go on and on but I picked just a few of the Libertarian Party goals in the 1980 Presidential campaign.

Let me say it this way, almost everything except having an Army, Navy, Marines & Coast Guard would go into the trash heap! Some of you are familiar with Ayn Rand. She was a Hollywood script writer who wrote books that caused some people to adopt libertarianism. It is a philosophy that preaches that every person has to make it on their own, without assistance from Government or even other charitable entities! I don't know everyone that is, or was, a libertarian but, as I understand it, many of the TEA PARTY CONGRESSMEN now in office are Libertarians. The Chairman of the Federal Reserve, Alan Greenspan who served from Reagan to Bush 41 to Clinton to Bush 43 was a libertarian. The reason I know that for sure was that Greenspan got Reagan to agree that Ayn Rand would be present when Greenspan was first sworn in as Chairman in the 1980's! He told people how much he admired Rand. Now, I'm not trying to paint libertarians as devils but it puzzles me how a strict proponent of libertarianism would be proud to head up the FED or Social Security or the EPA when all endeavors like that are contrary to the philosophy of libertarianism! The libertarians don't want government to regulate the Federal Aviation Administration much less oversee our capitalistic system! Guess who the candidate for VP of the United States of America was in 1980! It was David Koch, the billionaire who is pumping money into tea-party candidates. He is not evil either. If he is still the same Libertarian that he was in 1980, he is just trying to make as much money as he can possibly make and how much money you make or do not make is not his concern, if he is a true AYN RAND libertarian tea-party type conservative! ALTRUISM has left the room!

There is an ultra-conservative radio talk show host that is so hateful and "over-the-top" or, actually, "over the bottom" in most cases that I am not going to mention his name. I am not going to use his name but, he does exist. For the purpose of this book, I am calling him JOHN DOE.

When Supreme Court Justice Antonin Scalia died in a motel in Texas, John Doe came on the radio and said

"you just get used to this, 'Scalia found, it's natural, nothing going on here, He just died naturally," John DOE said, "And you're like, Whoa. Red flag. Then you realize, Obama is one vote away from being able to ban guns, open the borders and actually have the court engage in its agenda and now Scalia dies. I mean, this is hard core."…"I wonder if Clarence Thomas will die of a heart attack next week."…"Maybe they will kill Donald Trump next."

WHO do you think "they" is in the above quote? Other conservative talk and TV hosts chimed in and said: They did find a pillow over his (Scalia) face! While John Doe is a little more over the top, to say it softly, these are the kind of subjects that are quite prevalent in Conservative news radio, TV, newspapers and internet on a daily basis. This is the kind of NEWS that courses through the minds of millions of people every day, coming to them just like it did to me in my car as I drove from Northern Wisconsin to Missouri in the late 90's and 2000's. The only difference is that there is more of this kind of news today because radio, TV, iphones etc…have multiplied exponentially and newspapers have diminished. There are some people, when they hear this flagrant version of the news would say, "that's silly, no one would believe that!" But millions of people "buy in" to those types of stories. We live in a "reality show world", where people believe that those couples running through the jungle on TV could die at any minute, when they should be comforted that the camera crew would probably save them!

Seriously though, propaganda can be extremely dangerous. Goebbels taught us that lesson in the 30's and 40's in Germany. The German people, who are not a stupid people, became either stupid or afraid. After all, we have a black President who many believe is not only a muslim, but he wasn't even born in America. He never found his real birth certificate, did he? They don't believe he is a Christian! What causes this kind of propaganda in the year 2016? Just press the button on your device you are holding and someone, out there in the Cloud, will tell you the meaning of life! The question is, does that someone know anything beneficial to life?

LOBBYISTS BUY PROPAGANDA & GRIDLOCK

I enjoy the weekly program **60 Minutes** on television. I started watching it on a regular basis at least 30 years ago. When I tuned in on August 23rd, 2016 I noticed that Senator Tom Coburn was the guest of Lesley Stahl. I had heard of Senator Coburn and he was retiring because he was battling cancer. I hope he is making a great recovery!

However, I don't know that I ever heard a more depressing interview. It was an interview about ***GRIDLOCK!*** The segment wasn't titled gridlock but the subject discussed was pure and simple—gridlock! Senator Coburn was called the "Godfather of the Tea Party." He was also known as "Doctor No." Lesley and the Senator started out talking about the good relationship Coburn and Obama had when they were both freshman senators. Coburn says he "loves him as a man." They continued to be decent to each other when Obama became President but there was not much they agreed on. OK, I guess that's the way politics is.

Unfortunately, through his terms in the Senate, Coburn found every loophole in the Senate rulebook and became an expert in *blocking legislation* meaning that he could stop a bill long before it could be brought to a vote. When Lesley Stahl asked how many bills he blocked, Coburn said *thousands*! Lesley Stahl asked if he didn't realize that the Congressional approval rating in the Country was 7%! He agreed and said that "anybody off the street would do a better job" (in congress), meaning better than the people now in the Senate and the House. He also wondered "who are the 7% that think we're doing a good job?" and he and Stahl broke out laughing! He topped that comment off with suggesting, "let's get rid of them all and start all over again."

Thank goodness Stahl finally said, but "you are the reason for the gridlock." Coburn gave what might be the dumbest response in history. "No, no one knows about the holds!" Some of the legislation he held up were Veterans benefits, a paralysis bill and other Veteran related legislation. Thirteen Veterans groups attacked him! IF—if Harry Reid or Chuck Schumer had secretly blocked that legislation Cruz or Trump would be calling for severe condemnation of Reid or far worse. Steve Spalding of Common Core says about Coburn, "He's the number one champion of gridlock in the Senate!"

Now, you, Republicans and Democrats, can correct this injustice! Just because Coburn is retired, the game is not over. Just imagine, 100 Senators and their staffs, working for months to construct legislation and bring it to the floor for a vote, were wasting their time and millions of $$, not knowing that Coburn was going to block all of that work without the sun shining on it at all. There are 30 or 40 tea party--gridlock loving Senators and Congressmen still in office that possibly think just like Coburn. I believe, to honor the memory of his time in the Senate, the citizens of this Country should do what he recommended and "get rid of all of them," or at least the 30 or 40 Tea Party gridlock, just-say-no Congressmen and "start all over again!" It's the honorable thing to do! You Democratic voters have to help bring this about also. All of you voters reading this book remember, this was not my idea, it was Coburn's idea to "get rid of all of them!"

Congressman Paul Ryan is the new Speaker of the House. He undoubtedly doesn't agree with Senator Coburn because he would *have to go* also because Coburn meant both Senators and Congressmen. Here are the words of Paul Ryan to Chuck Todd on MEET THE PRESS on 12-20-15:

"We should not play identity politics as Conservatives or as Liberals which is a political tactic that aims at speaking to people in ways that divide them from one another. That is wrong in my opinion and both sides do it. I think it is wrong because all it will do is polarize us even further and we cannot have a unified Country if we keep doing that. So this is why leaders should lead to unify. This is why I am a Jack Kemp— Ronald Reagan—Happy warrior—Conservative!"

By mentioning Jack Kemp he is going back to Kemp-Roth and supply side economics and the quadrupling of our National Debt from 1981 to 1993 as delineated in chapter 2 of this book, so I will not repeat all of that again. On top of that, though, Paul Ryan is a libertarian. We saw in chapter 4 what libertarians believe in reviewing the 1980 Libertarian platform. In a simple review of Libertarian goals, they believe that Government should do as little as possible so the annual budgets of paying for government will be less and then we should reduce taxes on Corporations, the rich, the middle class and the poor. Some would say, that sounds GREAT! NOT if you analyze it!! Mitt Romney was right, the poor don't pay any Federal Income Tax right now but they do pay Social Security which they can't afford. The middle class has lost ground and are getting poorer. The millionaires and billionaires need to pay a higher tax and we have to raise the minimum wage to a living wage!

I heard a speech by a Republican presidential candidate Ted Cruz in the Milwaukee Republican debate talking about taxes and he said, regarding tax rates, that "we have to go back to Coolidge, Kennedy and Reagan and lower taxes".

Let me interject an author's note here because bringing up Kennedy, especially about taxes, is a common Conservative Republican ploy. First of all, they get to sound magnanimous because they threw in a Democrat in with 2 Republicans to sound balanced but you can see that Cruz is hard-pressed to find any Republicans in the last 100 years to brag about. Conservatives don't respect Kennedy but listing those 3 Presidents regarding their financial acumen is misleading in every way! Coolidge set the table for the Great Depression and Reagan-Bush41 quadrupled the total nation debt. Reagan's deficits and the supply-side debacle was a fiscal disaster for the Republicans but to listen to the candidates running for the Presidency, you have to conclude they missed class that day. A reporter said that in one Republican debate, some idea of the Reagan legacy was brought up 37 times! Yes, Kennedy cut taxes!!! From WW2 to 1961 the top rate was 91%. Truman and Eisenhower kept taxes high to pay off WW2 high deficits. With annual deficits finally corralled and the economy humming, Kennedy came in and cut the TOP RATE from 91% to 70%! If Cruz wants to emulate JFK and set the TOP RATE at 70%, <u>let the games begin!</u> It's rare when I want to do what Senator Cruz wants to do, but that just shows how affable and open-minded we liberals can be!

Whenever I think about Conservatives in Congress or the Senate, like Tom Coburn, wanting to block legislation and cut taxes, the name that jumps into my head is Grover Norquist. Earlier I said that Rush Limbaugh was the most powerful Republican since President Reagan's term with Drudge and Fox (O'Reilly & Hannity) close behind. By the way, I am mixing "apples and oranges" here. When I say, "most powerful Republican", I definitely mean EVERYONE: Presidents, Senators, Congressmen, talk show hosts, editorial

writers, TV "journalists", internet bloggers, you name it! The winner is still Limbaugh because of his longevity and the strength of his audience, but No. 2 is Grover Norquist.

Grover Norquist founded the "Americans for Tax Reform (ATR)." That organization opposes all tax increases as a matter of principle. Prior to the 2012 election, 238 of 242 House Republicans and 41 of 47 Senate Republicans signed ATR's "Taxpayer Protection Pledge" which requires the Senator or the Congressman to:

> "Oppose any and all efforts to increase the marginal income tax rate for Individuals and business and to oppose any net reduction or elimination of deductions and credits, unless matched dollar for dollar by further reducing tax rates."

Former Republican Senator Alan Simpson, certainly a Conservative and definitely not a shrinking violet, describes Norquist's position as, "no taxes, under any situation, even if your Country goes to hell." Some Republicans, who wanted to reduce the National Debt rather than increase it every year, also stated, like Simpson, that Norquist had become an obstacle to cutting annual deficits and the resulting National Debt.

Despite whether Simpson and other Republicans chose not to be in agreement with Norquist, it seems that a high number of Republican Senators and Congressmen sign on to the ATR pledge. As I understand it, it is a pledge that, if you violate it, there may be punishment. If you are a Congressman serving your first term and you violate your pledge, you may lose your support when you try to run again for office. Maybe people in the ATR or the Congress or the Republican Party will work against your reelection or the party will find another

Republican to run against you in the primaries even though you could win. This is a disastrous policy in my judgment, that is, disastrous for our Country.

Norquist, like his one-time mentor in the 1980's, President Reagan, is anti-government, a theme that streams through Reagan, Limbaugh, Norquist, Coburn, most Tea Party activists in the Congress and even some surprising names that we haven't mentioned yet. Norquist is quoted as saying, "I'm not in favor of abolishing the Government. I just want to shrink it down to the size where we can drown it in a bathtub." If we did what Norquist wants to do, I hope that all of today's and future voters, Republican, Democrat and Independent, are willing to say goodbye to Social Security, Medicare, the FDA, and similar benefits for the bottom 90% of our society!

Speaking of understanding, there are things about Norquist and his fellow Conservative travelers that I just don't understand. He is a smart person, an MBA from Harvard, the school that conservatives love to hate. He is an economist and an advisor to some foreign governments early in his career. It is said that President Reagan urged him to start his work that became the Americans for Tax Reform. But didn't Norquist see, like David Stockman did, that the trickle-down plan of cutting tax rates that were supposed to produce EVEN MORE *tax revenues* failed miserably from 1981 to 1992 and it took Bill Clinton and tax increases to turn the debt battleship around in the middle 1990's and even produce a miracle, that is, a balanced budget that Clinton gave to Bush 43 as a gift, but then Bush frittered it away like dust in a storm. I would have thought that Norquist would have been fiscally in love with President Clinton by the end of the 90's but I have never understood the conservative mind.

So far in this chapter, we have talked about the great gridlock politicians like Coburn and we haven't talked about Senator Mitch McConnell, the Republican majority leader, whose goal in life was the make certain that Barack Obama would not serve a 2nd term. We could talk about John Boehner but he is gone from the Speaker's job. He could not or would not get much legislation out of the House, evidently because of Tea Party gridlock. So, if Coburn, McConnell and others were blocking all progress in the Senate and Boehner and the whole Tea Party blocking in the House, Obama was fighting against a stacked deck. But if Obama wanted to get things done he had to use "executive privilege" and, like Rumpelstiltskin, he turned straw into gold!

What does Paul Ryan, the new Speaker of the House say in regard to this subject? At a Heritage Policy meeting in Washington, D.C., Ryan said:

"We cannot fall into the Progressives trap of acting like angry reactionaries, the left would love nothing more---they would love nothing more than for a fragmented conservative movement to stand in a circular firing squad and fire, so that the progressives can win by default. (on CNBC—Wed—02-03-16).

When Paul Ryan talks about circular firing squads, does he mean the Republican debates for the Presidency? The Democrats have no part in orchestrating that fiasco. Those debates have generated their own name calling, hatred and confusion in full view of the American people.

We have talked about the admitted gridlock and obstruction of Coburn, McConnell, Boehner and probably every member of the Tea Party—you know who you are. Now it's time to bring up the biggest obstructionists in the Country, namely, the **LOBBYISTS!** I am going to let the leader of the Presidential race in the Republican party, Mr. Donald Trump, introduce the lobbyists to you, my readers:

Trump says on the TV political show, "With all due respect", on 08-04-15:

"All of the lobbyists, many of which I employ or used to employ, and I know many of them, but they have tremendous power over these Candidates, (with the Kochs I called them puppets-*repeated by Trump*). They have tremendous power over these candidates and I'm not just talking about Kochs, I'm talking about lobbyists; talking about special interests. I'm talking donors. I was one of the big donors. I know the system. A lot of the time these candidates will do things that are very bad for the Country but they are good for the Company that the power group represents!"

So now that Trump has told us about how Lobbyists are used under the radar to get things done, let's explore how Republicans have used them to defeat causes since the 50's! There is a great book that I have just read titled, "Merchants of Doubt." In it's forward it states:

"How a handful of scientists obscured the truth on issues from Tobacco smoke to Global warming."

It charts the path of some talented but very conservative scientists that were drafted at first by the largest tobacco companies and then by Conservative "think tanks" to spread doubt about the health hazards of smoking cigarettes but then, over 4 or 5 decades the same modus operandi was used against issues like acid rain; the ozone hole; the EPA; and finally, the gorilla in the room, Global warming.

What do I mean by "doubt", you ask?" Let me explain it in steps to make it clear. In regard to cigarettes the steps were that the scientists that were hired would feed confusing data into the mix which would be fed to the deniers, then on to lobbyists, then to the politicians who could use it to slow or stop any legislation that would be detrimental to the tobacco companies. Here is the modus operandi:

Step one—(In the 1950's?) Cigarettes are wonderful! Haven't you watched Bogey and Bergman in Casablanca! They kiss and blow smoke in each other's face! The Marlboro man on that horse is impressive. He smokes all the time. He is a man to behold!

Step two—(years later) Don't believe those reports about smoking affecting your lungs and heart. Those government researchers are not capable of proper analysis. In fact, the government can't do anything right!

Step three—(years later) OK. There is a health concern here but let's not jump to any conclusions. It will take years of study and millions of dollars, IF, if the Congress will ever allocate any money to see IF smoking is really causing any problems.

Step four—(years later) Yes, it looks like cigarettes can cause cancer and other health problems. Maybe we could reduce nicotine or invent a magic filter! How about VAPPING!

Step five—(years later) Cigarettes cause cancer and other health problems. The party is over. Reality and knowledge have finally won!

The sad part of this story is that the tobacco companies and some of the researchers, lobbyists and politicians that blocked anything from getting done over 5 decades, knew in the 1950's, that there was strong evidence that cigarettes were detrimental to a person's health!

Can you, the reader, imagine anything worse? I can! Right now, today, our Country is going through the same sequence regarding Global Warming and the methodology and goals to play down and defeat the concept that Global Warming is happening to the USA and the Planet that we live on. It's easy to see that it is almost the identical steps are being taken that were used in the case of cigarettes, but this time the lobbyists and politicians are fueled by oil-gas-coal and companies related to energy!

Let's move right on to what I said was the gorilla in the room. No, I don't mean that Ted Cruz is a gorilla. He has already told us he is a modern day Galileo! Here is what he said about global warming proponents at Liberty College on 03-23-15:

> "What do they do? They scream, 'You're a denier.' They brand you a heretic. Today, the global warming alarmists are the equivalent of the flat-Earthers. It used to be {that} it is accepted scientific wisdom the earth is flat, and this heretic named Galileo was branded a denier."

The most significant part of Cruz's diatribe was that Galileo turned out to be right in his theory and Cruz is already wrong which will be unveiled in the next paragraphs. The sad part of his historical teachings for the students at Liberty College is that Cruz had the story wrong in the first place. The argument between the Pope and Galileo at the time was not about "flat-Earthers." It was about whether the earth was the center of the solar system as the Church taught. Galileo, who was instrumental in perfecting the telescope had concluded that the earth revolved around the sun.

So, Ted when you are 70 years old, as a profile in humility, you should go back to the students of Liberty College and admit you were wrong about every aspect of your "teaching-moment story" to them. We all hope that many informed and open-minded people will have been elected by that time who actually believe in science and do something to stop global warming so that you will still be on the planet and in good health when you are 70 years old.

When Pope Francis came to Washington at the invitation of the U. S. Congress and Majority Leader John Boehner, the Republicans were thrilled. They had tried to do this previously with Prime Minister Netanyahu of Israel and this would be another attempt to undercut the policies espoused by President Obama and it again would be done in Obama's own back yard, so to speak! It didn't turn out that way and I never have seen so many Republican Congressmen leave the Congress in such a grumpy mood. For a moment there, I thought the Pope was channeling Al Gore or Carl Sagan. The Pope made it clear that he believed from everything that he has read and observed that, in his opinion, Climate Change is a reality and some actions are needed to be taken. He was worried about drought and poverty causing displacement of millions across the world!

Jeb Bush, still running for President at that time, said on the evening news (06-18-15), "I respect the Pope, but I think it is better to solve this problem in the political realm." What kind of **jibberish** is that remark? The Pope wasn't saying that he knew how to solve the problem, no, he was positing that there IS a problem and maybe he was hoping that there were smart people out there that would take action to solve the problem. That brings me back to Cruz, who stated later in the Liberty College speech, "I'm a big believer that we should follow the **SCIENCE** and follow the **EVIDENCE**." On that point, I agree with Cruz. The following is the undeniable evidence:

Statement of the Department of Defense— Pentagon (23 July 2015)

"DOD recognizes the reality of climate change and the significant risk that it poses to U. S. interests globally. The National Security Strategy, issued in February 2015, is clear that climate change is an urgent and growing threat to our national security, contributing to increased natural disasters, refugee flows, and conflicts over basic resources such as food and water. These impacts are already occurring and the scope, scale and intensity of these impacts are projected to increase over time."

American Association for the Advancement of Science (2006)

"The scientific evidence is clear: global climate change caused by human activities is occurring now and it is a growing threat to society."

American Medical Association (2013)

"Our AMA…supports the finding of the Intergovernmental Panel on Climate Change's fourth assessment report and concurs with the scientific consensus that the earth is undergoing adverse global climate change and that anthropogenic contributions are significant."

American Meteorological Society (2012)

"It is clear from extensive scientific evidence that the dominant cause of the rapid change in climate of the past half century is human-induced increases in the amount of atmospheric greenhouse gases, including carbon dioxide (CO_2), chlorofluorocarbons, methane and nitrous oxide."

American Chemical Society (2004)

"Comprehensive scientific assessments of our current and potential future climates clearly indicate that climate change is real, largely attributable to emissions from human activities, and potentially a very serious problem."

National Aeronautical and Space Administration

"Ninety-seven percent of climate scientists agree that climate warming trends over the past century are very likely due to human activities and most of the leading scientific organizations worldwide have issued public statements endorsing this position"

Joint statement of 18 scientific organizations

"Observations throughout the world make it clear that climate change is occurring and rigorous scientific research demonstrates that the greenhouse gases emitted by human activities are the primary driver."

<u>Unanimously approved Comments</u>
195 Nations at Paris Accords (NYT-12-12-15)

"With a sudden bang of the gavel Saturday night, representatives of 195 nations reached a landmark accord that will, for the first time, commit every Country to lowering planet-warming greenhouse gas emissions to help stave off the most drastic effects of climate change. The deal, which was met with an eruption of cheers and ovations from thousands of delegates from around the world represents an historic breakthrough on an issue that has foiled decades of international efforts to address climate change."

"This is truly an historic moment," the United Nations Secretary General, Ban Ki-moon, said in an interview. "For the first time, we have truly universal agreement on climate change, one of the most crucial problems on earth."

President Obama, who regards tackling climate change as a central element of his legacy, spoke of the deal in a televised address from the White House. "This agreement sends a powerful signal that the world is fully committed to a low carbon future. We've shown that the world has both the will and the ability to take on this challenge."

I could go on with this "climate material" in enough volume to fill up some library shelves but if the information that is available right now and has been for years is enough to convince any real skeptic that Global Warming is real and ACTION has to be taken NOW or the USA and the world will pay a bigger penalty in the future. Are "deniers" too dumb and can't comprehend simple concepts like the Senator that brought a snowball onto the Senate floor session to prove that global warming was not real? That's almost like saying that I will never believe in global warming because it is cold out today! This Senator must be smart because his fellow Republicans made him the Chairman of the Senate Environment & Public Works Committee! What an irony that is! That could be the new basis for the phrase, "the fox guarding the chicken coop!"

On the other hand, is it possible that oil, coal and gas companies and their lobbyists are doing *anti-global warming propaganda* against pro-global warming realists? Is it possible that Senators and Congressmen who are "deniers" get rewarded with contributions for their reelection and promises of future employment. The Republican frontrunner, as I write this, Donald Trump, who I quoted earlier said: "They (the lobbyists representing companies) have tremendous power over these candidates."

While I am not voting for Trump, like in a Court case I offer up Trump's expert opinion about how Congress works regarding lobbying and I don't feel that I am being unfair to the "deniers" of global warming by citing that a possible future President of the United States believes that there could be incentives to the "deniers".

Voters must decide all these great issues in November of this year. But it can't be just a decision on who will be the President, although that is very important! Again, we must do what Republican Senator Coburn suggested. We know we cannot kick them all out because only a portion of the Senators are up for reelection each 4 years. But if we know the names of those Congressmen who are "deniers" of global warming and never do anything but oppose things, like the signers of the Grover Norquist pledge, maybe they should be gone, don't you think? You bright young college students, this would be a great project for you to work on and put your imprimatur on this election! Please, we beg you, do it for your Country!

9/11-THE PRELUDE TO WAR

> There are known knowns. There are things that
> we know that we know. There are known unknowns.
> That is to say, there are things that we know, we don't
> know. But there are also unknown unknowns. There
> are things we don't know, we don't know.

These were the words of Donald Rumsfeld, the Secretary of Defense, around the time we were invading Iraq on March 19, 2003. Some sources say that he had used these phrases in speeches previously in DOD and NATO speeches.

He was responding to questions posed to him about whether Iraq has "weapons of mass destruction" and our knowledge of where they are located. According to the March 30th ABC's program, THIS WEEK, Rumsfeld said, "we know where (WMD) they are. They are in the area around Tikrit and Bagdad and east, west, south and north somewhat."

Well, Mr. Rumsfeld, the belief that the WMD is either east, west, north or south, somewhat, that makes everything perfectly clear! From what you have stated, I believe that we are dealing here with a KNOWN KNOWN. That is you knew at that time that there were no "weapons of mass destruction" in Iraq and you knew that we would never find them when we invaded Iraq. Why do I think that, you ask?

Because it is widely observed in the Press that, starting with the GULF WAR in the early 90's, when Iraq invaded Kuwait and President Bush41 pushed Iraqi forces out of Kuwait, you and Wolkowitz, Perle, Cheney and other Republicans had been disappointed that President Bush41 didn't go all the way to Bagdad and take out Sadaam and you needed justification to do that now.

Starting back then, the idea of overthrowing Iraq was bought up by your group and to anyone that would listen, including President Clinton in the later 90's. It became easier to bring up the invasion to President Bush43, especially given the fact that Vice President Cheney was now in action and you and Cheney were joined at the hip. Years later, on March 18th, 2013, the Sunday Times interviewed another high official in the Bush Administration, Paul Wolfowitz. According to the Times reporting, Wolkowitz was a driving force behind the overthrow of Saddam Hussein and also conceded that a series of blunders by the Bush Administration plunged Iraq into a cycle of violence that "spiraled out of control." Wolfowitz also told the Sunday Times that he was the first senior official to advise Bush43, days after the September 11th attacks on the Twin Towers, to seek regime change in Iraq. In fact, Wolkowitz seemed proud of that recommendation. This was strange advice to give to the President given the fact that there was no connection that anyone knew about linking Iraq and Saddam Hussein with Osama bin Laden and the hijackers!

Before addressing the Iraq War, however, let's cover the issue of the horrendous 9/11 attacks on the Twin Towers and the Pentagon. There were 19 hijackers. 15 of them were from Saudi Arabia. 2 were from the United Arab Emirates. 1 each from Egypt and Lebanon. This is how ABC News tracked the leads up to 9/11 and the activities of the hijackers, the CIA and the FBI.

31 days before 9/11-Aug 11, 2001

President Bush is on vacation in Crawford, Texas, where 5 days earlier he had been warned by the CIA of a possible attack in a paper titled: "Bin Laden determined to strike in U.S." The document said al Qaeda members were believed to be in the U.S. and that a caller to the U. S. Embassy in the United Arab Emirates said "group of bin Laden supporters were in the U. S. planning attacks with explosives."

All 19 hijackers are, in fact, already in the U.S. on visas obtained under their actual names. On August 11, Hamza al-Ghamdi, who will be one of the hijackers in the second plane to hit the World Trade Center, buys a blue blazer at a Florida men's store. Osama bin Laden has approved the targets and is only awaiting final word on which day the attack will occur.

30 days before 9/11-Aug 12,2001

Al Qaeda recruit Zacarias Moussaoui has just arrived in Eagan, Minnesota, where he has moved to attend flight training school.

Some 70 FBI "full field investigations" related to Osama bin Laden are underway across the United States. None of them (my underlining) involve any of the 19 men who will commandeer passenger planes on September 11.

29 days before 9/11-August 13, 2001

Hijack leader Mohamed Atta and 2 other hijack pilots fly to Las Vegas for an apparent planning session. Marwan al Shehhi, who will take control of United Airlines flight 175 on September 11, purchases 2 black 4-inch pocket knives-the maximum allowable knive length under FAA rules at the time, from a Sports Authority store in Florida.

Zacarias Moussaoui begins flight training on a flight simulator at the Pan Am International Flight Academy in Eagan, Minnesota. He raises suspicions when he tells instructors that while he wants to learn to fly a 747 jet, he does not intend to earn a pilot's license. (author's note— follow that name—MOUSSAOUI)

28 days before 9/11-Aug 14, 2001

Mohamed Atta, Nawaf al-Hamzi and Hani Hanjour leave Las Vegas after an apparent planning session. Fayez Banihammad and Marwan al-Shehhi, who will hijack flight 175, withdraw $2000 from a Bank of America ATM in Lantanna, Florida.

27 days before 9/11-Aug 15, 2001

FBI agents initiate an "intelligence investigation" into Zacarias Moussaoui after flight school instructors report concerns that he might be a terrorist.

CIA counter-terrorism Chief Cofer Black tells a Defense Department convention, "we are going to be struck soon, many Americans are going to die, and it could be in the U. S.

26 days before 9/11-Aug 16, 2001

The crew of hijackers that will take control of American Airlines flight 77 and crash it into the Pentagon check in at the Valencia Motel in Laurel, Maryland, a few miles away from the headquarters of the National Security Administration, where operations are underway to detect suspected terrorists.

Using his FAA flight certificate, Hani Hanjour, who will act as pilot of the hijacked American Airlines flight 77, takes 1.3 hours of flight training at Freeway Airport in Mitchellsville, Maryland.

Zacarias Moussaoui is arrested on immigration charges as FBI agents in Minneapolis grow increasingly suspicious of why he enrolled in 747 flight training.

25 days before 9/11-Aug 17, 2001

Ziad Jarrah completes a "check ride," a test of piloting skills, with a flight instructor at Airborne Systems Flight School in Fort Lauderdale. On September 11, he will act as hijack pilot of United Airlines Flight 93, which the hijackers will attempt to redirect to Washington, D. C. It will crash in a Pennsylvania field after passengers revolt against the hijackers.

A deportation order is signed for Zacarius Moussaoui while FBI agents begin an effort to obtain a court order to search his computer.

24 days before 9/11-Aug 18, 2001

The FBI requests evidence of al Qaeda recruit Zacarius Moussaoui from a U. S. legal attaché in Paris to obtain a search warrant for Moussaoui's lap top computer.

Minneapolis FBI agent Harry Samit sends a memo to headquarters in Washington that Zacarius Moussaoui "is conspiring to commit a terrorist act." The memo goes unread by FBI personnel responsible for followup.

23 days before 9/11-Aug 19, 2001

A flight instructor at the Palm Beach, Florida County airport overhears Mohamed Atta on a plane radio shout in Arabic, "God is great!" Atta's name is in the airport log for August 19, 2001.

22 days before 9/11-Aug 20, 2001

Hani Hanjour, future hijack pilot of American Airlines flight 77, takes a flight lesson from an instructor who thinks Hanjour must have been trained by the military because he is able to navigate a plane without radar, using it's terrain recognition system. Hanjour shops Travelocity for flights on September 5, 2001 from Dulles Airport in Washington, D. C. to Los Angeles.

21 days before 9-11-Aug 21, 2001

Nearly $5000 is deposited in the United Arab Emirates checking account of hijacker Fayez Banihammad. The account is later used to buy tickets for Banihammad and another hijacker for United Airlines flight 175 on September 11.

A Jordanian in prison for suspected terrorism tells FBI agents of an impending attack against buildings in New York and Washington D.C., saying, "something big is going to happen." His credibility is questioned as he cannot provide details of time and place. FBI agent Margaret Gillespie learns for the first time that 2 known al Qaeda operatives have been tracked to the United States from Malaysia by the CIA, which keeps the information secret from domestic law inforcement agencies.

20 days before 9/11-Aug 22, 2001

FBI agents at the "Alec Station," a joint FBI-CIA station established to hunt Osama bin Laden, demand to know why the FBI was not notified by the CIA of the arrival in the U. S. of 2 known al Qaeda operatives, Khalid al-Mihdhar and Nawaf al Hazmi, in January 2000. United Airlines flight 93 hijack pilot Ziad Jarrah purchases a large color diagram of a 757 cockpit control system and a Garmin III Pilot GPS system for use on September 11.

19 days before 9/11-Aug 23,2001

CIA Director George Tenet receives a briefing about **Zacarias Moussaoui** titled, "Islamic Extremist learns to Fly," but no connection is made with the threat of an al Qaeda attack in the U. S. (What----??????!!!!!!)

The FBI begins an "unhurried search" (FBI phrasing) for two al Qaeda operatives reported to be in the U.S., Khalid al-Mihdhar and Nawaf al Hazmi. Florida suspends the driver's license of hijack leader Mohamed Atta for failure to appear in traffic court.

18 days before 9/11-Aug 24, 2001

Hijackers Khalid al Mihdhar and Nawaf al Hazmi are **finally put on the FBI's terror watchlist, 19 months after the CIA first tracked them to the United States.** (It was determined after 9/11 that the coordination between CIA & FBI was NOT exemplary.)

The attack date is set as the first 9/11 airplane tickets are purchased by hijacker Fayez Banihammad for United Airlines flight 175 from Boston to San Francisco.

A CIA cable describes **Zacarias Moussaoui** as a potential "suicide hijacker" involved in "suspicious 747 flight training."

17 days before 9/11-August 25, 2001

Hijack leader Mohamed Atta establishes an American Airlines profile and an Advantage frequent flier program number.

ONE DAY AFTER HIS NAME IS ADDED TO THE FBI'S TERROR WATCHLIST, HIJACKER KHALID AL MIHDHAR USES HIS YAHOO EMAIL ACCOUNT TO BOOK A SEAT ON AMERICAN AIRLINES FLIGHT 77 FOR SEPTEMBER 11. (*See above where CIA had tracked them to the USA 19 months previously*).

16 days before 9/11-Aug 26 2001

American Airlines flight 77 hijack pilot Hani Hanjour practices flight patterns with a rental plane from Congressional Air Charters in Gaithersburg, Maryland. Hijacker Waleed al-shehri uses his Visa debit card to book a first-class seat on American Airlines flight 11 for September 11.

15 days before 9/11—Aug 27 2001

American Airlines flight 77 hijacker Nawaf al Hazmi purchases a Leatherman Wave folding tool knife at a Target store in Maryland.

Hijack leader Mohamed Atta has a final planning session with the soon-to-be American Airlines flight 77 hijack team in room 343 of the Valencia Motel in Laurel, Maryland.

Following the FBI's inquiry, the Immigration and Naturalization Service revokes the visa of future hijacker

Khalid al-Mihdhar, but no request is made on an "urgent, emergency basis" to run the names of al-Mihdhar and fellow hijacker Nawaf al-Hazmi through INS data bases, which officials say, "might have been able to locate them."

14 days before 9/11-August 28 2001

Mohamed Atta buys tickets online for himself and another hijacker, Abdulaziz al-Omari, on American Airlines flight 11, which will be the first plane to hit the World Trade Center on 9/11.

Marwan al-Shehhi, the hijacker of United Airlines flight 175, buys his ticket for 9-11 from the United ticket counter at Miami International Airport.

13 days before 9/11-Aug 29 2001

United Airlines flight 93 hijacker Ahmed al-Haznawi reserves his ticket for September 11 on Travelocity.com, while brothers Hamza and Ahmed al-Ghamdi reserve their tickets for United flight 175.

United flight 93 hijacker obtains a Virginia driver's license from the DMV in Springfield, Virginia, using the address of illegal immigrant Luis Martinez Flores. Flores has already allowed two other hijackers to claim they live at his address.

12 days before 9/11-Aug30 2001

Hijacker Ziad Jarrah books his ticket for United Airlines flight 93.He also attends kickboxing and street-fighting classes at a gym in Hollywood, Florida—skills he will later use to storm the flight's cockpit.

Mohamed Atta purchases a utility tool kit containing a large knife from Lowe's. On September 11, Atta and the other hijackers will slit the throats of passengers and cabin crew members on American Airlines flight 11.

11 days before 9/11-Aug 31 2001

American Airlines flight 77 hijacker Hani Hanjour makes his reservation for 9/11, the last of the hijackers to do so. He pays in cash since the ticket costs $1842—too much to charge on his debit card.

Hanjour and Nawaf al-Hazmi close each of their Hudson United Bank accounts, while Hamza al-Ghamdi and Ziad Jarrah end their leases in Florida. The hijackers will spend their remaining nights in hotels and motels.

10 days before 9/11-September 1 2001

Waleed al-Shehri purchases a silk shirt and khaki pants at Burdines Department store in Pompano Beach, Florida. The hijackers will be dressed in Western clothing on September 11.

Hani Hanjour moves out of his Paterson, New Jersey apartment. His landlord returns the full deposit in cash without inspecting for damage because, as he later tells the New York Times, Hanjour "was a gentleman."

9 days before 9/11-September 2 2001

Hani Hanjour returns to Laurel, Maryland, where he and the other American Airlines flight 77 hijackers will remain until the day of the attack. Three of those American flight 77 hijackers obtain weekly guest passes at Gold's Gym in Greenbelt, Maryland, paying in cash.

8 days before 9/11-September 3 2001

The hijackers are 8 days away and the hijackers remain undetected. The 4 hijackers who will actually fly the planes have, by this day, finished a round of test flights at small airports and will all have FAA pilot's licenses.

In Germany, Mohamed Atta's fellow hijack planner and roommate Ramzi bin al-Shibh receives $1500 via wire from an al Qaeda bank account in the Mideast. He apparently uses the money to evacuate Germany, but is later arrested in Pakistan.

Intelligence officials in Egypt say they warned the U. S. on this day of an impending al Qaeda attack. President Hosni Mubarak says the warning involved an airplane or an Embassy.

7 days before 9/11-September 4 2001

Hijack leader Mohamed Atta sends a Federal Express package to an accomplice in the United Arab Emirates, returning several thousand dollars in unused cash.

Senior Security officials at the Federal Aviation Administration are finally told by the FBI that a suspected terrorist by the name of **Zacarias Moussaoui** may have been training to hijack a 747 aircraft at Kennedy Airport in New York. The FAA does **NOT** issue any additional security alerts.

After requesting an immediate meeting months earlier, Richard Clarke finally meets with National Security Advisor Condoleeza Rice and othe administration officials to discuss the al Qaeda threat against the Uited States. That same day, Clarke issues a memo urging officials to imagine hundreds dying because of the governments reluctance to pursue al Qaeda.

After resigning from the FBI, al Qaeda expert John O'Neil begins his new job at the World Trade Center. He will die on 9/11.

6 days before 9/11-September 5 2001

American Airlines flight 77 hijackers Hani Hanjour and Majed Moqed are photographed using an ATM at the First Union National Bank in Laurel, Maryland. At the Sun Bank in Florida, where several of the hijackers have accounts, Fayez Banihammad wires more than $8000 to an al Qaeda account in the middle East, returning money he no longer needs.

In Paris, FBI and CIA officials attend an emergency session at the French Ministry of the Interior. The Americans are given information on the bin Laden ties of **Zacarias Moussaoui**, *but his case remains on the FBI back burner.* In Washington, Congress returns from it's summer recess and the Senate Intelligence Committee holds a hearing about terrorism at which bin Laden is discussed.

5 days before 9/11-September 6 2001

2 American Airlines flight hijackers, Abdulaziz al-Omari and Satam al-Suqami, fly from Florida to Boston and check in at the Park Inn.

In Afganistan, Osama bin Laden receives word the hijacking are scheduled for the following Tuesday, September 11.

United Airlines flight 175 hijacker Mohand al-Shehri calls United airlines to inform them that his first name was spelled incorrectly on his reservation for 9/11.

4 days before 9/11-September 7 2001

The hijackers of United Airlines flight 93 fly from Florida to Newark, New Jersey, where they will spend their remaining nights at the Marriott Hotel at Newark International Airport before boarding their planned flight to San Francisco on the morning of the 11th.

3 days before 9/11-September 8 2001

Atta wires $7860 to the Wall Street Exchange Center in Dubai from the Giant and Safeway stores in Laurel, Maryland. Several of the hijack ringleaders, including Ziad Jarrah and Mohamed Atta, go to dinner at one of their favorite restaurants, the food factory in Laurel Maryland.

2 days before 9/11-September 9, 2001

Mohamed Atta flies from Baltimore to Boston, where he meets up with United Airlines flight 175 hijacker Marwan al-Shessi. The two spend the night at the Milner Hotel in downtown Boston.

In the early hours of the morning, after leaving dinner in Laurel, Maryland, United Airlines flight hijacker Ziad Jarrah receives a speeding ticket in Maryland as he heads north on I-95 at 90 miles per hour.

Ahmad Shah Massoud is assassinated by two suspected al Qaeda bombers posing as journalists, who used documents forged by Osama bin Laden's chief lieutenant, Ayman al-Zawahiri. FBI agent Ali Soufan says, "Bin Laden is appeasing the Taliban. Now the big one is coming." The 5 American Airlines flight 77 hijackers cook and eat a meal in the kitchenette of their Laurel, Maryland motel.

1 day before 9/11-September 10 2001

Mohamed Atta, likely trying to stagger the hijackers arrival to Boston's Logan Airport on the day of the attacks, makes a last-minute decision to drive to Portland, Maine with Abdulaziz al-Omari, where they will catch a connecting flight to Boston at 6 A.M. on September 11.

Outside Washington at the Headquarters of the National Security Agency (NSA), electronic intercepts pick up conversations between 2 suspected al Qaeda leaders. One reads, "The match begins tomorrow"; the other, "Tomorrow is zero day." The conversations will **NOT BE** translated and transcribed until **September 12!**

SEPTEMBER 11ᵗʰ, 2001

The terrible attack takes place. Atta and 4 hijackers hit ONE WORLD TRADE CENTER. Minutes later, Al-Shehhi and 4 others hit TWO WORLD TRADE CENTER. Hanjour and 4 others crash into the PENTAGON in Washngton. Jarrah and 3 other hijackers are rushed by heroic passengers but the plane crashes near Shanksville, Pennsylvania before the passengers could overcome all of the hijackers. Since this plane only had 4 hijacker's and the others had 5, could it be that **ZACARIUS MOUSSAOUI,** arrested in Minneapolis almost a month before 9/11, was slated to be the 5ᵗʰ hijacker on this plane and if he had been followed day and night, rather than being arrested, he might have led FBI & CIA to all the players?

On September 14ᵗʰ, 3 days after 9/11 with debris still smoldering, President Bush went to the Twin Towers site and, with his arm around a fireman, said this:

America today is on bended knee—In prayer for the people whose lives were lost here—For the workers who worked here—For the families who mourn. The nation stands with the good people of New York City, New Jersey and Connecticut—We mourn the loss of 1000's of our citizens—**I HEAR YOU!—ALL THE REST OF THE WORLD HEARS YOU**—and the people who knocked down these buildings will hear from all of us soon!

KICKING OVER THE HORNET'S NEST

We have heard President Bush's words at the site of the Twin Towers disaster. At the very moment of that speech, something very dramatic was happening that I don't believe was ever reported on the evening news until much later.

In his speech Mr. Bush used the phrase "the people who knocked down these buildings," but he did not say WHO they were. Now, I am not suggesting that he should have told the Nation that he knew or suspected that the buildings were knocked by Muslim al Qaeda terrorists led by Osama bin Laden. I am also not suggesting any conspiracy theories on the part of President Bush and others.

However, the reader should move his mind back to 9/11 and the days following. ALL airlines were grounded. No planes, I said, ZERO planes were allowed to fly in or out or inside the Country in the 3 days after 9/11. Finally, almost 3 weeks later, on September 29th, the New York Times wrote a story with these headlines:

Fearing Harm, Bin Laden Kin Fled From U. S.

"In the first days after the terror attacks on New York and Washington, Saudi Arabia supervised the urgent evacuation members of Osama bin Laden's extended family from the United States, fearing that they might be subjected to violence.

In his first interview since the attacks, Saudi Ambassador Bandar bin Sultan, also said that private planes carrying the Kingdom's deputy defense minister and the Governor of Mecca, both members of the royal family, were grounded and initially caught up in the F. B. I. dragnet. Both planes, one jumbo jet carrying 100 family members, and the other 40, were eventually allowed to leave when airports reopened and passports were checked."

Mr. bin Laden is estranged from his family. One of his two brothers in the United States called the Saudi Embassy frantically looking for protection. The brother was sent to a room in the Watergate Hotel and told not to open the door. Most of bin Laden's relatives were attending high school or college. They are among the 4000 Saudi students in the United States. King Fahd, now deceased, sent an urgent message to his embassy here saying there were "bin Laden children all over America" and ordered, "Take measures to protect the innocents," the ambassador said. When I read that King Fahd has said that, I thought of all those innocents that died on 9/11 at the Twin Towers, the Pentagon and Shanksville, even some small children.

Who do you think had the time and the authority to oversee this emergency transfer of 140 Saudi's out of the USA when our whole Country was on lockdown? Certainly the President, the Secretary of Defense, the FBI and the CIA had to be in the loop, don't you think? Do we have a list of all the Saudi's that left? We didn't know where Osama bin Laden was the day after 9/11, did we? Even though Osama was supposed to be alienated from most of his relatives, isn't it possible that some of the 140 people we allowed out could have been supportive in finding Osama or giving other information about Al Qaeda that was supposed to be their enemy also! Or on the opposite side, is it possible that 1 or 5 or 10 of those

Saudi's might have given some assistance to the hijackers in the form of money or help in the United States?

I am going to bring politics into it for a moment. What would right wing republicans say if all of the above happened when Barack Obama was President? According to pollsters, a high % of the Republican party think Obama is a Muslim. I am sure that IF he had been President at that time, talk radio and Fox would have set accused Obama of far more than than his Religious affiliation!

I am going to write about War now because it is, unfortunately, an important part of history that we have to try to understand and hopefully will teach us all lessons to use in the future. I am not an expert on war but in my military studies to get a commission in the U. S. Navy, I had the opportunity to study military history.

I honor our Veterans and I am very aware of the sacrifices they made. Just before my brothers were in the service, there were older friends of theirs that would lie about their age to get into the service and go fight the Japanese at IWO JIMA or in Europe at the BATTLE OF THE BULGE. These soldiers should never be forgotten. But just because a person fought in a war doesn't mean it was a "good" war or a "just war", but every fighting man should be honored because he did his duty with honor when he was called to do so.

Before getting into the wars in Afganistan and Iraq, both of which followed the 9/11 attacks and were purported to have something to do with Osama bin Laden, I want to bring up a definition of WAHHABISM which will be pertinent to the rest of our discussion about war. For more than two centuries, Wahhabism has been espoused in Saudi schools called Madrassas. It is an austere form of Islam that insists on a literal interpretation of the Koran. Strict "Wahabbis" believe that all those who don't practice their form of Islam are heathens and enemies. Critics say that Wahhaabism's rigidity has led it to misinterpret and distort Islam, pointing to extremists such as Osama bin Laden and the Taliban.

The creator of this Muslim philosophy, Abd al-Wahhab demanded conformity that was to be demonstrated in physical and tangible ways. He argued that all Muslims must individually pledge their allegiance to a single Muslim leader. Those who would not conform to this view **should be killed, their wives and daughters violated, and their possessions confiscated.** The list of apostates meriting death included the shite (shia), sufis and other Muslim denominations, whom Abd al-Wahhab did not consider to be Muslim at all.

Abd al-Wahhab's advocacy of these ultra radical views inevitably led to his expulsion from his own town and in 1741, after some wanderings, he found refuge under the protection of Ibn Saud and his tribe. What Ibn Saud perceived in Abd al-Wahhab's novel teaching was the means to overturn Arab tradition and convention. *It was a path to seizing power!*

Their strategy, like that of ISIS (or Daish) and the Taliban today was to bring the peoples who they conquered into submission. They aimed to install fear!

Unless this author and the reader and the American people understand the complexities of Wahabbism and the part that it plays in Muslim countries, we will never be able to understand what role the U. S. should play, if any. There are 24 Countries in the middle east and Africa that are predominately Muslim. The population of all of them is "majority Sunni" except for Iran, Azerbaijan, Lebanon and Iraq. But the nations that have been associated with Wahabbism and Isis and the Taliban are our great "friends", Saudi Arabia, Afganistan and Pakistan. I am calling them friends because they have been the recipients of our blood and our money over the years. The Saudis get arms from us and we covet their oil. The Pakistanis get financial aid from us and they are a Muslim country with atomic weapons. We have been helping the Afghans for years, even building schools and roads, also helping them fight the Taliban, whether they want us to do so or not.

I believe that Saudi Arabia and Pakistan have the most Madrassas in the middle east. Sixteen of the nineteen hijackers on 9/11 were young Saudis and I believe the other three hijackers were Sunnis too. When it was ordained in the Madrassas that **"those who would not conform to these views should be killed",** they didn't just mean other muslims, they also meant those people in New York, in the Twin Towers! When you can convince young students that it would be a wonderful thing if, when you reached your 20's or so, you should go kill yourself and many other people and you will be rewarded in death with 72 virgins in the hereafter. That is not a philosophy that would attract me to their cause, but I guess if you're taught that by your Madrassa and your parents second the motion, you could be considered a "convert."

Before we go further I want to make a disclaimer. While Madrassas are most prevalent in Sunni countries, I am certainly not condemning all Sunnis. But I am perplexed about the fact that America's greater enemies seem to be the Shite (Shia) countries like Iran and Lebanon! I understand why the U. S. and Iran are at odds today, especially with their very disturbing proclamations regarding what they would like to do to our friends in Israel. But I'll bet that few Americans remember what great friends we were with Iran when we overthrew their government and put the Shah in power decades ago.

Saddam Hussein, was probably not a "wahabbist" Sunni, but he did rule with an iron fist keeping Iraqi Shites and Kurds in fear. Not many Americans remember that in the

1980's, Donald Rumsfeld went to Iraq and made an "arms deal" with Sadaam because Iraq was fighting a war against Iran and we wanted to help him. I wonder when Sadaam found out that we were already shipping arms to Iran during the same period. Those transactions were covered in earlier chapters of this book.

So these are risky liaisons, Sunnis and Shites distrust each other. Neither of them trust Americans either and from what I have stated above, there are reasons for those feelings. Right now, there is a constant debate about "putting boots on the ground." Before we do that we should look to our right and left and ask, "who do we trust?"

THE WAR IN AFGANISTAN

Mullah Omar was a Mujahadeen fighter who had taught at a Pakistani <u>madrassa.</u> After that war he returned to Kandahar, Afganistan and founded the Taliban. Then, in 1996, bin Laden, who had been in the Sudan, came to Afganistan also. He cooperated with Mullah Omar but al-Qaeda maintained it's own training camps but supported other organizations. Keep in mind that bin Laden was the money source to maintain camps and pay soldiers (terrorists). So the Taliban and al-Qaeda were coexisting during this period.

On August 7, 1998, truck bombs struck two U. S. Embassies in Nairobi, Kenya and dar es Salaam, Tanzania. A total of 200 people were killed, 12 of them Americans. It was an al Qaeda operation. President Clinton ordered missile strikes on terror training camps in Afganistan. The international community imposed sanctions on the Taliban, calling for bin Laden to be surrendered to the U.S. CIA Special Activities Division Paramilitary teams were active at the time to capture or kill Osama bin Laden.

Then, after 9/11, Osama bin Laden and al Qaeda would move up the target list, although not high enough for some people. Other people were talking about invading Iraq for some reason. Of course they had been talking that way since the early 90's.

But only 3 months after 9/11, members of the British Special Boat Service (SBS) team listened in to conversations on a captured short wave radio and they heard a voice believed to be Osama. The CIA pinpointed bin Laden's location to within 10 meters. Forty U. S. Special Forces fighters raced to kill bin Laden. Keep in mind, the U. S. was working with the British and also 100's of Afgan soldiers.

When they reached an outcrop they saw a large group estimated at 900 al Qaeda fighters and the battle for Tora-Bora began. The team called in airstrikes over the next 56 hours. Remember, this was mountainous country and Osama was in a cave some of the time. After 3 days, some of the Afgans said, "Osama has gone to Pakistan. We arc going home." We don't know for certain that Osama actually escaped or had some Afgan "friends." He was killed 10 years later by U.S. Special Forces.

We still have troops in Afganistan, 15 years after 9/11. The Taliban and some al Qaeda are still there. Pakistan, a Country with madrassas and the nuclear bomb, is still our "ally", but coexists with the Taliban. It is a confusing world.

THE IRAQ WAR

This war is going into it's 13th year. If I tried to relate the War's complete story in prose and paragraphs, it would be as long as Tolstoy's "War and Peace," although not quite as good. Instead I am going to give you "historical bullet points" which should bring the incidents into a chronological perspective.

- On February 5, 2003---Colin Powell addresses the U.N. Security Council. He delivers a 10 page presentation with video and audio of trucks and warehouses. It didn't convince all of the people the Bush Administration wanted to convince, especially some European Allies. Later, It will be shown that George Tenet contributed to the report with information that fell short of being accurate, to say the least. However, showing loyalty and solidarity with their own government, many U. S. politicians and citizens gave a reluctant "GO" to President Bush.
- March 20, 2003---President Bush goes on TV and announces the start of the Iraq war. I remember watching the gigantic explosions which I believe included an area of buildings where Sadaam Hussein was located. He was not.
- The advance is quick and Bagdad is soon under American control. Statues of Sadaam are toppled and there is some cheering for American troops. Soon the looting of the city begins.
- May 1, 2003---Under a banner of MISSION ACCOMPLISHED on the aircraft carrier Abraham Lincoln, off the California coast, President Bush declares that is "one victory in a war on terror that began on September 11th, 2001 and still goes on."
- May 2003---President Bush appoints Paul Bremer to head the Coalition Provisional Authority in Iraq. He is like an "interim President" to run the Country until an Iraqi government can be put together. He announces two policies that will will cause future disaster and they were:

1.) De-Baathification of the government. The predominately Sunnis who worked in the Sadaam government were members of the Baath party. These people would lose their life's work. Some of them

were teachers or administrators or hospital workers. Their livelihood was threatened.

2.) The Iraqi military was dissolved. 100's of 1000's of Army troops were out of a job. They would go home with their uniforms, rifles, pistols and anything else they could get their hands on. They were very angry. Within 72 hours of Bremer's orders, the car bombing and truck bombing started. Car and truck bombing would become a signature weapon of the war.

— August 19, 2003---A suicide bomber drives a cement truck into the side of the United Nations compound in Bagdad killing 17 people and wounding at least 100. Among the dead is Sergio de Mello, the United Nations secretary general's special representative in Iraq.

— December 13, 2003---Sadaam Hussein if found outside of Tikrit and he is arrested without incident. He is literally in an 8 foot hole and is haggard and dirty after 9 months on the run.

— June 28, 2004---The White House had a new plan—GET OUT! The military retreated into large, fortified bases. The focus was on an exit strategy. Set up a governing council, establish a constitution and let the Iraqi's govern themselves. Bremer left on the 28th, 2 days ahead of schedule because of security concerns. They were so worried about Bremer's flight out that he boarded a airliner, waited 15 minutes until the crowd was gone, walked out another door of the plane, boarded a helicopter, flew over to another small plane, boarded a smaller airliner to Jordan, got out and flew another plane to the United States.

- December 15, 2005---Millions of Iraqi's cast ballots to elect a parliament to a our year term.

- Until February 22, 2006 there had been sporadic car bombings and violence against Shites by Sunnis coming in from Anbar province. By now, there were al Qaeda fighters that had come in to help the Sunnis and Iranians were helping the Shites. Al Qaeda forces, eager to start a civil war, pushed the Shites over the edge when it destroyed the Al-Askari Mosque in Samarra, one of Shia Islam's holiest sites. Over the next 10 days, Shia militia's took their revenge, massacring Sunnis. In Bagdad, their death squads moved house to house, killing as they went!

Note: Eventually the American Government pays Al Sadr and his Shia army $331,000,000 (yes—331 million $) in "reconstruction money" for the Mosque.

- April 22, 2006---Shite leaders select Kamal al-Maliki as their nominee for Prime Minister. He will be Iraq's first leader since Sadaam. He was President Bush's pick.

- Summer of 2007---Bush has put General Petraeus in charge. He is a counterinsurgency specialist. The SURGE BEGINS with 30,000 new troops in the mix. American and Iraqi losses are heavy each month in the Fulugia area. Petraeus reaches out to the Sunni (enemy) leaders and convinces them to stop attacking American troops and focus only on battling Al Qaeda, who have been fanning the flames of this Civil War.

The United States ended up paying approximately **$400,000,000 (yes- 400 million) in bags of cash to the Sunni leaders so that 103,000 Sunni soldiers known as the "Sons of Iraq" or the Awakening, would stop attacking Shites and car bombing American positions. At almost the same time, Muqtada al-Sadr, the head of the Shia militia, called for a ceasefire and stopped attacking coalition forces. He already had his 331 million (above)!**

The confluence of those three factors, the Surge, the "Awakening" and Sadr's ceasefire, reduces the violence in Iraq to a low grade insurgency. Hoping to maintain that "progress," President Bush signed an agreement with Maliki ensuring that American troops remained in Iraq through 2011.

Before President Bush left office, he flew to Bagdad for a Press conference. While there, standing next to Maliki, an Iraqi journalist took off his shoes and threw them at him. I understand that "throwing shoes" is a big insult in the Muslim world. Both Bush and Maliki were very disturbed by this incident. Bush left town as quickly as he could.

What he should have done is grab Maliki by the collar, stare into his eyes and say: **"In the future, starting TODAY, unless you treat Sunnis and Shites with mutual respect and make them equal citizens of your Government, this Government in Iraq will be a disaster."**

Whatever was said, that wasn't done. Malaki had Sunnis arrested and killed. Some Sunnis left the Country. Violence picked up again. The 103,000 Sunnis in Anbar that previously was Sadaam's army now dominated Sunni home territory in areas north and west of Bagdad. They were now rich and well equipped. The new Shite Iraqi army was just the opposite and they were going to prove that by "cutting and running" and leaving all the trucks, guns and hardware on the road as a gift to the Sunnis. Soon, the Sunnis would begin car bombing again, coming into Bagdad to kill Shites and Americans.

THE CIVIL WAR WAS IN FULL BLOOM!

**SOON IT WOULD EXPAND INTO
THE DESERT OF SYRIA!**

**THERE WERE NO WEAPONS OF
MASS DESTRUCTION!**

OBAMA INHERITS
RECESSION & WAR

I will not apologize for being repetitive because I am trying to expose the **facts** to the American voter prior to the upcoming election. If you look at the first paragraph of chapter 2 of this book, President Reagan brings up the subject that I am hammering away at now! In the 1st part of his 1st inaugural address he states:

> "For decades, we have piled deficit upon deficit, mortgaging our future and our children's future for the temporary convenience of the present. To continue this long trend is to guarantee tremendous social, cultural, political and economic upheavals."

He must have believed strongly in the dangers of "deficits upon deficits" to say those words as the first thoughts from him to the American people. Why then, did he do what he did by cutting taxes under Kemp-Roth and buy in to the "trickle down, Laffer-curve economy," that proselytizes the more you cut tax rates on the rich and on Corporations, the more total tax revenues will increase because the economy will grow faster. Reagan must have believed that, but it not only didn't happen that way, instead, it was a deficit disaster. Let me illustrate how bad it was:

From the formation of our Country in 1776 to the end of the Carter Administration in 1980, 205 years of history through 39 Presidents the Total

accumulated NATIONAL DEBT in 1981 was---
$ 998,000,000,000 (998 bill(rnd)
When Reagan left after 8 yrs., he added:
$ 1,694,636,512,032(1 trill-695 bil)
When Bush41 left 4 yrs later, he added:
$ <u>1,462,302,943,460</u>(1 trill-462 bil)
Total National Debt when Bush41 left:
$ 4,154,939,455,492(4 trill-155 bil)

A prominent Republican at a recent Republican debate said that Barack Obama will have run up a bigger debt in his 8 years than all the Presidents in the history of our Country. I didn't write down his name but I have heard several Republicans say similar things in debates. Too bad they missed that day in political science class or was it arithmetic? Ronald Reagan almost **tripled** the National Debt (**of ALL other Presidents before him**) when he ended 1988 at 2 trillion-692 billion (rounded). But your efforts at misleading the voter are hereby duly noted! Obama will give it a shot, but Reagan-Bush41-Bush43—NOT Clinton, have set too high a bar! I will talk about the "multiplier-effect" in deficits later in this chapter.

Let's talk about the subject of misleading the public. Congressman Paul Ryan, as Speaker of the House, is the third most powerful politician in our Country. As you know, he is third in line of succession after the President and Vice President. The following are some comments he made on CNBC which is a network primarily dedicated to financial news and the stock market. John Harwood was the interviewer:

Ryan—What we need is a clarifying election in this Country to ask the men and women who are citizens of this nation to break the impasse. We have a broken, divided government that isn't fixing the big problems facing our Country and if we keep this broken, divided, big government going as it is, these problems get out of control. They go beyond our ability to fix them on our own terms, ...

Harwood (breaks in)- "So what do you do if a democrat wins the Presidency?"

Ryan—Let me finish my point. What I believe we do is we take an agenda of the Country and say: This is what we think we need to do to fix this Country's big problems. This is how we prevent a debt crisis. This is how we grow the economy and then, we let the Country make a decision. If we win the kind of election that we are hoping to win in 2016, not unlike what Ronald Reagan and my mentor, Jack Kemp, did in 1980, then we will have earned a mandate from the Country to put these things in place."

Pause by Ryan—"if then, in your (Harwood's) scenario----

Harwood—"you hold the House and a Democrat is President."

Ryan—"Then we have a divided government. Then we're just going to figure out how to make it work. But I think it's going to be more of the same. That's the frustration. What we're worried about is having more of the same, which is all of these big problems facing our Country. They are piling up. They are still fixable. If we have another Presidency, like this Presidency, then I really do worry that our best days are behind us and that's the problem. If we have a divided government, we are going to have to figure out how to make it work and it won't be nearly as good as if we had unified government to fix these problems."

Gosh, Paul Ryan, even though I'm a former "cheesehead," I am really confused. You say, "we have a <u>broken, divided</u>

government!" Why is that, Paul? Is that because your 30 or 40 Tea Party Republicans stood in the way of anything that the Democrats or even some Republicans wanted to pass? Is that because there is hatred for Obama in this Congress that even goes beyond your statement:

"If we have another Presidency, like this Presidency, then I really do worry that are best days are behind us." Did you know that, Paul, that President Obama has rather high approval ratings, certainly many times that of the House!

Did you know about the interview between Lesley Stahl and Senator Tom Coburn featured in chapter 5 of this book. Senator Coburn was bragging about blocking 1000's of bills over his career, before they hit the Senate floor and how proud he was that he did that work. When Stahl asked Coburn if he knew that the Congressional approval rating in the USA was 7%! Coburn knew that it was 7% and he wondered to Stahl, "who are the 7% that think we are doing a good job?" Then both Coburn and Stahl broke out laughing! Then Coburn said, "let's get rid of all of them and start all over again." Paul, do you agree with that?

Then there is Senator Mitch McConnell whose goal in life was to do everything he could do to stop President Obama from being reelected in 2012. There are lots of negative thoughts in the air. Does McConnell ever think about doing great things, do you think?

So, Mr. Ryan, you say we have a broken Government, but I think that 93% of the American people believe that we have a broken Congress. That's not all your fault but you certainly want to fix it. Your predecessor, John Boehner, couldn't fix it. His own republican Tea Party people seemed to block him every time, something like Senator Coburn did in the Senate. You and some of your people have to learn to become "ball carriers," rather than just "blockers" of all progress.

You want to go back to the 80's and the "Reagan legacy" as you and other Republicans call it a few times each day. I don't mind that as long as you don't make the same kind of mistakes that Reagan did. But maybe, if you transferred back to the 1980's in your mind, you could morph into the mind of Democratic Congressman Tip O'Neil from the 80's. He supposedly <u>cooperated</u> (Sorry to throw that foreign word into the sentence) and together they got things done, even extending Social Security. Oh, I forgot myself for a moment. I should have remembered that you are a Libertarian so you might not be a supporter of Social Security and other Federal programs like that, even though those programs put a safety net under the poor and middle class. If America did not have Social Security today, in 2016, we would be in a world of hurt. Millions of people today, who are living paycheck to paycheck or even Social security check to SS check, would be out on the street without Social Security. Some of your conservative friends don't believe that or, they believe SS should be optional. The fact that it is NOT optional is the <u>essence</u> of the Social Security program! You are a smart person! Don't you see that? If it were optional, most of the very people who need SS to get by in retirement would have optioned NOT to be in the program in the first place.

So, if Mrs. Clinton wins, you "really do worry that our (the USA) best days are behind us." What you should think, if you were a Paul (Tip O'Neil) Ryan positive thinker, that I am going to do my best to cooperate and find common ground with this great Democratic President! Like Tip O'Neil, the American people would think of you as a great Speaker, a great person and a great American!

As I finish his book, I wanted to get away from talking about our economy and debt problems, even though they are very important. I also feel obligated to address President Obama's part in the debt issue since Republicans have made an effort to blame everything on him, which as you will see, is baseless.

Four Presidents, in the last forty years since President Ford, have played a part in contributing to the 19 trillion $ debt that we might have when President Obama leaves office. {Note: I have made a record of Annual Budget Deficits, by year and by Presidential term and that record is in appendix 1 in the back of this book. The figures are from the Congressional Budget Office (CBO)}. By the way, historically we almost always run annual <u>deficits.</u> In the 100 years that this book is about, I believe only Coolidge, Truman and Clinton had <u>surpluses</u>, but I did not research that aspect and could be wrong. Here are some examples of the chronology of debt:

— In President Carter's 4 year Presidency, his average yearly deficit was $74,060,000,000.(74 billion-60 million). This is consistent with deficits thru the 60's and 70's with normal inflation. Back to Carter's $74,060,000,000 deficit average. Reagan came into office, cut taxes and deficits started skyrocketing. In 1986, Reagan's deficit for just that one year was $302,199,616,658 (302 billion-200 million(rnd), a bigger deficit than all four years of deficits in the Carter years. For the first time in a 200+ years of American history we were dealing in the trillions, not just billions.

(NOTE---rnd after numbers means rounded.)

The irony was, then, President Bush ascended the throne. He inherited the same kind of bad stuff that he, himself, called "voodoo economics" when he ran against Reagan in

1980. He ran on a pledge, "no new taxes", but he was falling into the abyss of debt so he raised taxes, but his party didn't get behind him 4 years later. So, in just 4 years, he ran up an average of 365.6 billion dollars per year for a total of $1,462,302,943,460 (One trillion-462 billion (rnd). The Country that was less than 1 trillion when Carter left office was now at 4.2 trillion as Clinton took office.

As we progress through time, 3 things are at play here. They are:

1.) The "battleship in the water" problem.
2.) Inflation.
3.) Interest on the debt.

1.) When Bush41 followed Reagan, Bush inherited large annual deficits that had been increasing almost every year in the Reagan years. This is not a problem you can solve in your first year, if at all. Bush raised taxes, but that was too late and you can't immediately cut spending that you and your predecessor had just put in place. It's very hard to stop a battleship in the water!

2.) Inflation- This is obvious. Things almost always cost more year after year. That bomber that cost $150,000,000 in 1985 might cost $600,000,000 today.

3.) Interest on the debt- If the total national debt was less than 1 trillion in 1980 and will be pressing 5 trillion in 1993, then the interest on the debt, which has to be paid each year as part of the budget, will possibly be 5 times as much.

In economics, a multiplier effect is an effect that says that future debt will grow faster because of those 3 elements. So, in Bush's last year, 1992, the annual deficit was a few dollars short of 400 billion. If Clinton stayed in office for 8 years and even if he keep deficits at a yearly 400 billion (stopped the battleship), he would still add 3 trillion—200 billion to the runaway debt! Unlike his two predecessors, Clinton raised taxes and didn't get into any big wars. In his second year (1994), he slowed down the battleship and each year except one, deficits were lower after that. In Clinton's last year, 2000, the total deficit was $17,907,308,271(17 billion-907 million) which I believe is scored as a surplus by CBO because it is a surplus when adjusted for inflation and scored as a % of GDP. John Kasich has bragged about it in Republican debates because he was in Congress at the time. Kasich also said the Bush43 could have inherited big surpluses from Clinton going into the 2000's. The "battleship in the water" can work in the *surplus* direction if an exceptional President precedes your term and you have the smarts to take advantage of his inertia! It didn't happen that way!

When President Bush43 came into office, he did a strange thing. He pulled a Paul Ryan! Instead of believing his Dad about "voo-doo trickle-down economics," he bought into the "Reagan legacy." It was a disaster for the Country, but why are we surprised! In Bush's last year alone(2008), he hit a $ 1,017,071,524,650 (1 trillion-17 billion(rnd). It took 205 years (1776 to 1980) for the total national debt to accrue to just short of 1 trillion and Bush beat it in one year. The total national debt was now $ 10,124,821,196,882 (10 trillion—125 billion (rnd).

But Bush43 didn't just give a 10 trillion—125 billion present to Obama. He gave him the worst recession in 80 years since the Great Depression of the 1930's. On top of that he gave Obama two wars, Afganistan and Iraq, which is where Bush kicked over the hornet's nest. The people we "saved" from Sadaam Hussein, the Shites and Sunnis of Iraq, were now in Civil War and ISSIS was forming from the remnants of the Sunni Baathists that we had run out of Bagdad early on. Soon they would include Syria in their destruction.

In the recession, millions of people in the USA were out of work. But the world was in recession also and many Countries around the world are still in trouble since the 07-08 crash. Before 07-08, Wall Street thought up new algorithms called "credit default swaps" and sold them to banks around the world. Our rating agencies like S & P and Moody's gave these swaps high credit ratings when it appears that there were only about 20 people on Wall Street or anywhere in the Country that had a clue about what these financial instruments were worth.

The world was in chaos from war and financial institutions were going down the drain. The biggest banks and auto companies had to be bailed out. The debt was about to grow above a trillion a year and any tools to "stop this battleship" in the water had disappeared. This is the situation that President Obama stepped into in 2009! What was the plan of Republican leaders? Block progress-block-block-block! Could Obama balance the budget? Could he save the economy? Could he put people back to work? Could he end the wars in progress? Could he help the middle class and poor in this Country. Will Senator Colburn, John Boehner, Paul Ryan and all those Tea Party congressmen quit negative thinking and help the Country avoid the worst consequences of this greatest test to our Country since the great depression and WW2? Can pigs fly?

On 03-23-06 President Obama was in Argentina to meet their new leader. At an open news conference a reporter asked a question that may answer some of the questions in the last paragraph. I am going to ask President Obama to end this chapter and this book for me! I don't know President Obama and this book is not written for the Democratic party. Only my wife and children know that I am writing it and they are amazed that I have finished it.

The reporter at the Argentina press conference asked Obama: "What was your dream when you got elected and were you able to realize it?

Obama—(In short, press conference type phrases).

- I ran for office because I believe deeply in the American people.
- and that our politics did not fully reflect all the values and the talents and the goodness of the American people.
- I thought I might be able to align our Government with our ideals. To make sure that every child has opportunity. To make sure that if people get sick, they can get healthcare.
- To make sure we don't discriminate against people on the basis of race-or gender-or disability-or sexual orientation.
- That we are good stewarts for our planet-That we grow an economy so that everybody benefits-not just a few at the top.
- I won't say that we've got 100% done, but we've got a lot done. It is indisputable that the economy is much stronger then when I came into office. We've created over 14,000,000 new jobs.
- We.ve cut the annual fiscal deficit by 2/3rd. We've provided health insurance to 20,000,000 people who didn't have it before.
- We have not only reduced our carbon footprint, we have led the way to gain a global agreement on carbon change.

- On the international front, Cuba is just one example of the work we've done. The Iran nuclear deal that took away that threat from the World but also gave Iran the opportunity to join the community of nations.
- Work in Afganistan ending a war, but giving them the opportunity to secure their own future. Work in remote places, like Burma, where there had been a 40 year military junta, has now been on the brink of a new era of democracy.
- So, I think our values, the values that I felt best represented America, have also been represented in our foreign policy.
- One of the things I learned after 7 ½ years in office and I've used this metaphor before, we're like a relay runner. When we take the baton, we're behind in the race. We don't always choose the circumstances of when we get the baton. But I ask—did we gain ground when we had the baton—did we advance the causes we care about—I believe we achieved that.
- I certainly have not been successful in getting the two parties to work together more cooperatively and the tone of our politics doesn't reflect what is best in us.

The author's final words are:

PLEASE VOTE IN 2016--RELY ON FACTS—AVOID PROPAGANDA

THE END

APPENDIX 1

Total National Debt by Presidency

*All data is taken from the Congressional Budget Office

(note---bil means billion—tril means trillion---rnd means rounded)

Note: From the beginning of our
Country (1776) thru the term of
President Carter, the Total
Accumulated National Debt
of the 39 was Presidents
Was..........................$ 998,000,000,000 (998 bil-rnd)

After President Reagan's term,
1981-1988 inclusive.........$ 2,692,636,512,032 (2.7 tril-rnd)

After President Bush's term,
1989-1992 inclusive........$ 4,154,939,455,492 (4.2 tril-rnd)

After President Clinton's term,
1993-2000 inclusive........$ 5,764,487,009,857 (5.8 tril-rnd)

After President Bush43 term,
2001-2008 inclusive......$10,124,821,196,882(10.1 tril-rnd)

After President Obama's term,
2009 to 2016 inclusive...$ NOT FINALIZED---(18.6 trillion?)

Annual Deficits by Presidential Year

Reagan—1981---	$ 90,154,000,000 (rnd)	Bush43—2001 ---	$133,285,202,313
1982 ---	144,179,000,000	2002 ---	420,772,553,397
1983 ---	235,176,000,000	2003 ---	554,995,097,146
1984 ---	195,056,000,000	2004 ---	595,821,633,587
1985 ---	250,837,000,000	2005 ---	553,656,965,393
1986 ---	302,199,616,658	2006 ---	574,264,237,492
1987 ---	224,974,274,294	2007 ---	500,679,473,047
1988 ---	252,060,821,088	2008 ---	1,017,071,524,650
Bush41—1989 ---	255,093,248,146	Obama—2009 ---	1,885,104,106,599
1990 ---	375,882,491,590	2010 ---	1,651,794,027,380
1991 ---	431,989,899,920	2011 ---	1,228,717,297,665
1992 ---	399,317,303,824	2012 ---	1,275,901,078,829
		2013 ---	671,942,119,311
		2014 ---	1,085,887,854,036
		2015 ---	326,546,285,750
		2016 ---	**Not finalized yet.**
Clinton-- 1993 ---	346,868,227,618		
1994 ---	281,261,026,874		
1995 ---	281,232,990,696		
1996 ---	250,828,038,426		
1997 ---	188,385,072,262		
1998 ---	113,046,797,500		
1999 ---	130,077,892,718		
2000 ---	17,907,308,271		

Author's note: Readers should notice the "battleship in the water" multiplier effect in the above numbers. Every President has to pay a price for the deficits the previous President was running! I have already explained that, in President Carter's four years in office his average annual deficit was $74,000,000,000 (74bil). Reagan topped Carter's 4 years in just one year (1986)! As you can see above, Bush41 pushed huge deficits onto Clinton, who pushed miniscule deficits onto Bush 43, even Kasich bragged about that in a debate! Then Bush 43 pushed the first TRILLION $ DEFICIT in a single year onto Obama in 2008---along with the 2nd greatest recession in 100 years and two wars to fight and finance! The debt battleship was in the water and moving fast. Obama has finally slowed it down. Bottom line is: <u>Every Republican President—Reagan-Bush 41-Bush43 practiced trickle-down & raised the National debt at a fast pace & every Democratic President –Carter-Clinton-(especially)& Obama slowed it down!</u>

Printed in the United States
By Bookmasters